FROM LILLIPUT TO LORD'S

FROM LILLIPUT TO LORD'S
GREG YOUNG

SilverWood

Published in 2017 by SilverWood Books

SilverWood Books Ltd
14 Small Street, Bristol, BS1 1DE, United Kingdom
www.silverwoodbooks.co.uk

Copyright © Greg Young 2017
Images p61, p62, p63, p65, p67 © Ken Piesse Cricket Library
Images p61, p64, p65, p66 © Getty Images | Dr Andrew Britto

The right of Greg Young to be identified as the author
of this work has been asserted in accordance with the Copyright,
Designs and Patents Act 1988 Sections 77 and 78.

All rights reserved. No part of this publication may be reproduced,
stored in a retrieval system, or transmitted in any form or by any means,
electronic, mechanical, photocopying, recording or otherwise,
without prior permission of the copyright holder.

ISBN 978-1-78132-628-2 (paperback)
ISBN 978-1-78132-629-9 (ebook)

British Library Cataloguing in Publication Data
A CIP catalogue record for this book is available from
the British Library

Page design and typesetting by SilverWood Books
Printed on responsibly sourced paper

CONTENTS

	Prologue	9
One	A Brief History of Early Barbados	19
Two	The Development of Cricket in Barbados	25
Three	The 'W Formation'	36
Four	The 1950s – A Great Decade…	45
Five	Why the Dominance of Bajan Test Batsmen…	68
Six	Frank Worrell and the 1960s	82
Seven	Bajan Test Players From 1950 to 1960	91
Eight	The Legacy of the Bajan Greats of the 1950s	140
	Epilogue	147
	Appendices	148
	Bibliography	156
	Acknowledgements	161

No country in the world has been as totally addicted to the game of cricket as Barbados […] Suffice it to say that West Indies cricket has owed more to Barbados over the years than to any other country.

R Goble and K Sandiford

It was Lilliput cricket that was responsible for transforming Sir Garry Sobers into such a great player. Sobers did not have the money to buy the costly kit or go for training. Lilliput cricket used to be played [in Barbados] on small patches of ground by the poor. All that was required were three sticks and a ball rolled in tar. Sobers' mother used to make the ball and also chip out a bat out of a two-and-a-half feet long piece of wood. This is the hard way the man came up.

Hilaby Drakes

PROLOGUE

The past is never dead. It's not even past.
William Faulkner

14 December 1960. Shadows lengthen across the Brisbane Cricket Ground. Wesley Hall is about to bowl the final ball of a Test match between the West Indies and Australia. The last Australian batsman is at the crease, scores are level and either side can win. The West Indies need one wicket and Australia need one run. Australian captain Richie Benaud would later recount that he had never seen players and spectators gripped with such a frenzy at a cricket match.

In the midst of the unbearable tension, Frank Worrell, captaining the West Indies in a Test series for the first time, calls Hall over and says, "Wesley, I'm watching you. And what is more, the Empire is watching you too. One ball to go and if you bowl a no-ball, you will never be able to land in Barbados again!"

The players, the four thousand people at the ground and the hundreds of thousands of fans around the world who are glued to their radios are about to experience the most exciting finale in Test cricket history.

On the previous day journalists had predicted an Australian victory, but the West Indies refused to accept defeat. Worrell continually urged on his players and convinced them that they could win. The West Indies fought back and by lunch on the final day it looked as though the game would be drawn. Some journalists had already left the ground to catch early flights home. But over the next two hours Australia crumbled to 6 for 92 and it looked as though the West Indies may conjure an unlikely win. There were further twists to come. With half an hour remaining Australia needed only 27 runs to win.

> I wrote of the last half hour of this Test that if a writer of books for boys had been idiot enough to invent it his publishers would have beaten his brains out with his own manuscript [...] No author, however insensitive, would dare to rupture reason with such fictional fantasy.
>
> *JS Barker*

With two overs remaining Benaud and Alan Davidson were at the crease and Worrell was still calmly reminding his men to relax and concentrate. The batsmen met for a mid-pitch discussion and agreed they should not take any risks. Benaud pushed the next ball to the right of Joe Solomon at forward square-leg and called for a run. Solomon gathered the ball, threw down the stumps and Davidson was run out for 80. In the Australian dressing room the next batsman Wally Grout fumbled nervously for his kit, having mislaid his batting gloves. Swearing, he stood up and realized he had been sitting on them.

"This was to be the most melodramatic over ever bowled, an over that raised blood pressures beyond surgical limits!", wrote Gordon Ross, executive editor of *The Cricketer*. "If a whole book were ever to be written about one over alone, then this is the one."

Hall's first ball hit Grout a painful blow on the thigh, but the batsmen managed a sharp single. Five runs needed from seven balls. Years later in an after-dinner speech, Hall humorously recounted the stress of bowling the final over:

> The captain called me over and said, "Wesley, I'm still watching you. Whatever you do now, *do not* bowl a bouncer at Richie Benaud." I said, "OK, skipper, you just watch me." But as I walked back I had other things in mind. I became very purposeful. If

I could just get this man now, four and half million people in the West Indies would really come awake; and since it was only about three in the morning, that would have been a good achievement. I found that there was a little pep in my step and a little spring in my heels. So, forgetting all that the captain had said, I bowled the fastest bouncer that I'd ever bowled in my life. Benaud, feeling surprised, shaped for the hook. It took the glove and then Alexander was triumphantly in the air, taking the catch and rolling over in great triumph. I swung round, my arms raised, going towards my captain, hoping he will embrace me. But all I got was a stony silence and a wicked stare. So I said, "He's out, skipper, he's out!" Frank Worrell said, "What did I tell you? Do you really understand what would have happened had that ball taken the top edge and gone for four runs?"

Five runs needed from six balls, with two wickets remaining. New batsman Ian Meckiff blocked the third ball. He swung and missed at the fourth ball down the leg-side and found Grout bearing down on him, looking for the strike. Wicketkeeper Alexander threw the ball to Hall, who flung it at the stumps at the bowler's end. Only Alf Valentine's desperate dive saved four overthrows. Gideon Haigh described Meckiff's recollection of the scene:

> It was pure bedlam. Wally was practically on top of me, shouting to run, and I hadn't moved. Wes had got the ball from Alexander: he was in the middle of the pitch and he literally could have strolled to the bowler's end and run me out but he let fly and missed.

Four runs needed from four balls. Australian and West Indies players joined each other in the dressing rooms and shouted or hushed, according to the moment; a moment invariably changed with the next ball bowled.

Hall knew that Grout could play the hook shot well and was probably hoping for a bouncer, so he could finish the game off with one shot. Hall disguised his fifth ball, dropping it on a good length, and Grout's cramped shot lobbed towards square-leg. In the heat of the moment, Hall twisted sharply from his follow through and sprinted after the catch, but he hadn't seen Rohan Kanhai standing perfectly positioned. Hall tried to take evasive action but his elbow struck Kanhai's head and the ball spilled to the ground. In anguish, Hall moaned, "The good Lord's gone and left us!" Worrell, showing neither distress nor annoyance, patted the distraught Hall on the back and replied, "Forget it, Wes."

Three runs to win from three balls, with two wickets remaining. Hall's next delivery was waist-high on leg stump and Meckiff pulled it to deep mid-wicket. The ball stopped a yard short of the boundary, where Conrad Hunte swooped on it as the batsmen attempted a third run. Hunte rifled a ninety-yard return to wicket-keeper Alexander, who whipped off the bails to run out the diving Grout.

One run to win from two balls, with one wicket remaining. Lindsay Kline tried to appear confident as he walked to the pitch, but Worrell saw through the facade and said, "You look a little pale, Lindsay." Kline thought the scores were tied as he approached the crease but most of the West Indians thought Australia was two runs short of victory. "Run for anything," Meckiff told Kline. "It doesn't matter where the ball goes, just run."

Wes Hall later recalled the moment when Frank Worrell warned him about bowling a no ball:

> It was then that I saw the predicament I was in. And Frank Worrell, as cunning as he is, called me over as I made my way back and says, "I have nothing to tell you. But the batsman doesn't know that I have nothing to tell you. So if I move the man at backward square-leg two feet to the left, then two feet to the right, the batsman wouldn't know that I have nothing to tell you." So he did just that. There was Joe Solomon, two feet to the left and then two feet to the right.

Hall describes the last ball:

> I made my last lonesome trek back forty yards away from the stumps. As I came in, gasping for air, pressing through for the last ball, my foot planted some three yards behind the crease, just in case we had a benevolent Australian umpire.

Kline glanced the ball just wide of square leg and the batsmen set off for what looked like the winning run. But Joe Solomon had gathered the ball cleanly. Yelling at teammate Peter Lashley to move out of his way, Solomon underarmed the ball from side-on and threw down the stumps. Every West Indies' fielder screamed an appeal at square leg umpire Col Hoy, who later recalled, "He was miles out […] There was no one there."

The Test was over, but no one knew the result. Spectators flooded onto the ground as the West Indies players were celebrating, but Worrell was shouting, "No, we haven't won!" It was just after 4.00am in Barbados when a radio station anchorman mistakenly announced to tired listeners that the West Indies had won by one run. In the dressing room West Indian Gerry Gomez grabbed Australian Norman O'Neill in a bear hug and shouted, "We've won, we've won," to which O'Neill replied, "Wait a minute, I think we've won."

Not even the scorers were sure. After much deliberation Australian journalist Ray Robinson, who had been sitting with the scorers, announced that it was the first tie in Test history. At 6.30pm Ian Meckiff still didn't know the result. Cradling his head in his hands he moaned, "Fancy losing like that," to teammate Colin McDonald, who set him straight about the result.

Benaud went on to the field to greet Worrell and they walked off with their arms around one another's shoulders. The spectators massed in front of the dressing rooms, chanting, "We want the West Indies." Wes Hall recounts that everyone – umpires, players, those who were not playing, those who were out and the extras – gathered in the one dressing room, where they celebrated until late that night. The Australian selectors were enthralled by the match, Sir Donald Bradman telling Benaud, "This is the best thing which could possibly have happened for cricket."

> Professional cricket writers are, by and large, a hard-bitten lot. Watching cricket is their job and they are as likely to get emotional about it as a plumber about fitting a new washer on a bathroom tap [...] Only once have I seen the press-box boys rise as one man to give an ovation to cricketers. That was at the end of the Brisbane test in 1960.
>
> *JS Barker*

The tied Test was a triumph of leadership by Frank Worrell, the first captain to succeed in welding the brilliant individual West Indian players into a disciplined team. Richie Benaud later told Worrell that it was the greatest game he had ever experienced, played the way cricket should be played. Sir Jack Hobbs, one of *Wisden*'s five greatest Test cricketers of the twentieth century, celebrated his seventy-eighth birthday during the tied Test. "The tie in Brisbane," said Hobbs, "is the best possible birthday present I could have had."

Trinidadian historian, political activist and cricket writer CLR James wrote that Test cricket was in a 'decadent' era prior to the 1960/61 series between Australia and the West Indies. Captains were only looking to avoid defeat, batsmen just wanted to remain at the wicket and bowlers just wanted to avoid being hit around. Only months before the tied Test, England and the West Indies had played in a Test series which commentator Tony Cozier described as 'uninspiring'. The pitches had been over-prepared and both sides had tried to wear down the patience of the opposition batsmen by serving up fast, short-pitched bowling interspersed with nagging spin bowling coupled with defensive fields. There was no urgency to the play, scoring rates rarely climbed over three runs per over and the average over rate was fourteen per hour.

Commentators and former players had expressed their concerns about the future of the game. Benaud recalled that before the start of the tied Test Sir Donald Bradman, as Chairman of Selectors, had asked if he could attend the pre-Test team meeting and put a point or two to the Australian players. Bradman told the players that the Australian team of 1960/61 could lead the way to one of the most attractive cricket series seen in Australia, but that it was up to them. He added that the selectors would choose players who were playing good cricket and would look 'in kindly fashion' on players who played aggressively and were clearly thinking about those who pay their money at the turnstiles. This impressed the Australian players, several of whom had been together through the 1950s and witnessed cricket which they would not have wanted to pay their money to watch.

Frank Worrell was of the same view, having already decided to restore to the 1960/61 series the spirit of the game he had learnt in Barbados. Benaud's response was just as positive and the result was the most exciting Test series anyone could have wished for. At the conclusion of the final Test in the series at the Melbourne Cricket Ground, a match that had swayed to and fro until the final hour, more than two thousand spectators gathered at the entrance to the players' enclosure chanting, "We want Frank."

The Australian Cricket Board of Control gave the West Indies team a farewell dinner, at which it was announced that a trophy, to be named the Frank Worrell Trophy, would be presented for future competition between Australia and the West Indies. It was the first time Australia had ever honoured an international cricketer in such a way.

Such was the West Indies' performance and conduct on the tour that they were given a ticker tape parade through Melbourne, cheered by a crowd of more than one hundred thousand people. Former West Indies Test all-rounder Sir Learie Constantine said of the parade:

> For the first time in history Australia has paid tribute to a visiting captain by lining the street, some with tears in their eyes from sheer ecstasy, while the more sophisticated clapped and cheered for the contribution that Frank Worrell had made to the greatest series of Test matches.

Worrell reflected:

> As we travelled though the milling crowd at a snail's pace, we heard tremendously gratifying statements from the sporting Aussies…but the statement which was quite frequently made and which brought a lump to my throat and tears to my eyes was: 'Come back soon!' […] It was ironical for me to hear for the first time in my career: 'Come back soon!' Every time I think of these words my heart grieves.

Australian commentator Alan McGilvray believed that although the West Indies did not win the series they earned respect as a cricketing power and Frank Worrell deserved the lion's share of the credit. He became a father figure to his players — something which wouldn't happen again in West Indies cricket until the emergence of Clive Lloyd as captain fifteen years later.

The 1960/61 series in Australia concluded an era which was classified by author and former Jamaican Prime Minister Michael Manley as the second of four periods of West Indies cricket. The four periods Manley described were 1928–1939: the age of George Headley and Learie Constantine; 1947–1960: the age of Everton Weekes, Frank Worrell, Clyde Walcott, Sonny Ramadhin and Alf Valentine; 1960–1974: the age of Garry Sobers, Rohan Kanhai, Wesley Hall and Worrell's great captaincy; and 1975 to the time of Manley's book, which would subsequently continue until the mid-1990s.

The fourth period was a golden era, when the West Indies Test sides conquered all before them. From 1980 to 1995 the West Indies were undefeated in twenty-nine consecutive Test series, during which they played 115 Tests and lost only fifteen. Clive Lloyd, Vivian Richards and Richie Richardson all won more than forty-five percent of the games they captained, while losing twenty-five percent or less. Richards retired in 1991 having never captained the West Indies in a losing series.

On that point, Bajan author and social commentator Grantley

E Edwards noted a tendency of some modern cricketers to make disparaging remarks about the generations before them, while failing to recognise that those generations built a foundation and left a proud legacy. 'They seem unaware that their very existence is due to Everton Weekes and the many others that went before,' wrote Edwards:

> They seem ignorant of the fact that the cricketing house which they currently inhabit was built by these founding fathers. [...] Hence they are painfully unaware of the glorious tradition of the West Indies brand of cricket, which is the Barbados brand. [...] The trend was set whereby it is believed that this brand of West Indies cricket magically appeared from the sky and that there was just a cricketing void before the late 1970s and 80s…

In his foreword to *Fire in Babylon*, Clive Lloyd stated, "In my playing days I always felt the shade from the branches of our cricket family tree. I believe its roots are deeper and stronger than those of all the other cricket-playing nations. I knew that Rohan Kanhai and Garry Sobers had learned from Frank Worrell and that he in turn had taken good things from the example of George Headley and Learie Constantine. When it was my time to lead the side, the knowledge that there were links in the chain to which I was connected was an invaluable source of strength."

Lloyd named Sobers, Worrell and Kanhai as sources of inspiration. These players dominated in the second period, during which the West Indies defeated England in a Test series for the first time on English soil and were finally led on a permanent basis by a black captain. "It is difficult to deny that the West Indies are now the supreme cricketing nation in the world", wrote AA Thomson in the mid-1960s. "The foundation of this supremacy was laid in 1950 with almost terrifying efficiency."

In the second period the West Indies announced to the cricketing world that they had arrived as a confident and dominant force. And for the duration of that period one tiny island in the eastern

Caribbean produced magnificent West Indies Test cricketers – some of the greatest to have played the game – in numbers disproportionate to its size and population.

The island from which those players hailed is Barbados, the smallest of the cricket-playing nations. In the eighty-eight-year history of West Indies Test cricket, eleven West Indian players have been knighted. Six of those players were born in Barbados and all six played Test cricket during the second period.

Barbados celebrated its fiftieth anniversary of independence on 30 November 2016. In recognition of that event this book examines the historical importance of cricket in Barbados and the factors that led to the island becoming such a powerful influence in West Indies cricket, and pays tribute to the Test cricketers who made Barbados famous in its pre-independence days.

ONE

A Brief History of Early Barbados

> How a man's heart swells within him when he first sees the kindly land beckon to him over the salt waves!
> *Henry Coleridge, describing Barbados in the nineteenth century*

Barbados is the easternmost island of the main Caribbean archipelago, its nearest neighbouring islands lying over one hundred miles to the west. Barbados's western coast of idyllic beaches is lapped by the turquoise Caribbean Sea and its rockier and wilder eastern coast battered by Atlantic winds and surf. Unlike many other Caribbean islands, Barbados is neither mountainous nor made of volcanic rock, but mainly flat and composed of corallite rocks. It has no major rivers or lakes and its only regular supply of fresh water is from the rain that filters through the porous limestone. Barbados is small; twenty-one miles long, fourteen miles at its widest point and 166 square miles in area. It is roughly the size of the Isle of Wight, with a permanent population of around 280,000 people.

In 1625 the Anglo-Dutch supply ship *Olive Blossom,* captained by Englishman John Powell, broke its journey home from America by landing at St James Town (now Holetown) on Barbados's west coast. Powell found the island uninhabited by humans. The French had never made it to Barbados and the Spanish hardly seemed to have suspected its existence, lying as it does so far east of the main island chain. It is thought that peaceful Arawaks once inhabited Barbados but had been annihilated by war-like Caribs, the Caribbean 'master race' who were reputedly so bloodthirsty that their name became corrupted into 'cannibal'. But despite their ferocity the Caribs too were hunted, by Spanish slave-traders, and it is likely that they abandoned Barbados to avoid capture. Powell erected a cross with the inscription 'for James K of E and this island' then departed for England.

In 1627 Powell's younger brother, Captain Henry Powell, landed at St James Town with eighty English settlers and ten African slaves to settle Barbados. By 1639 the settlers had established the Bridgetown Assembly, the third-oldest parliament in the British Empire after those of Virginia and Bermuda.

From the time of settlement Barbados was intensely loyal to the English Crown. Author and Bajan resident Julian Armfield wrote that during the English Civil War between the Cavaliers of King Charles I and Oliver Cromwell's Roundheads, a substantial number of Englishmen from both sides fled to Barbados. An uneasy peace was preserved in Barbados during the early years of the conflict on the simple basis that the sugar planters, referred to as the 'plantocracy', had a common interest of growing rich.

This situation changed when Cromwell had King Charles I beheaded in 1649 and Francis Lord Willoughby arrived in Barbados in the following year, as Lieutenant-General. Willoughby summoned an assembly, which passed an Act acknowledging the King's right to the sovereignty of Barbados. The Council and Assembly of Barbados promised to support Willoughby and published a declaration, in which they set forth their determination to defend Barbados in the name of His Majesty and to preserve the liberty they enjoyed under their constitution.

The Royalists in Barbados, headed by Willoughby, proclaimed Charles II as their king and began a reign of terror against the Roundheads. Cromwell sent a fighting force to Barbados, under the command of Sir George Ayscue, consisting of seven ships carrying a thousand soldiers and several hundred guns. Ayscue's fleet arrived off Barbados in October 1651 and anchored in Carlisle Bay and Oistins Bay, constituting the first invasion of Barbados since British colonisation. But although Ayscue had two thousand troops he could not effect a landing. Sixty longboats manned with troops commenced storming the Fort Royal, but were forced to retreat in the face of a Royalist cannon barrage.

Ayscue sailed his fleet up and down the west coast, mounting attacks on the Royalists at night. After several months he had created a blockade, which prevented Barbados from trading with the outside world. But Ayscue had his own problems. He lacked the resources to mount a full invasion and there had been a severe outbreak of scurvy among his men. The Royalists, by the same token, were unable to drive the Roundhead fleet away, resulting in a deadlock. In the end Ayscue, knowing his position to be precarious and wanting to avoid the destruction of the island, consented to Willoughby's demand for a treaty.

In January 1652, after a siege lasting three months, Barbados capitulated to the parliament and the Charter of Barbados was signed. Cromwell maintained control of Barbados while allowing the Royalists to internally self-govern. The Barbados government would consist of a governor, a council and an assembly to be chosen by a free and voluntary election of the freeholders. No taxes, customs or excise would be laid, nor would any levy be made on any of Barbados's inhabitants without their consent. And all laws that had been made by the island's general assemblies not repugnant to the laws of England would remain valid.

It did not take long after settlement for Barbados to prosper financially. 'Tiny Barbados […] It was here that England's earliest expressions of imperial hunger and inhumanity led to the crime of mass enslavement of Africans', wrote West Indian historian Sir Hilary Beckles:

> It was also here that English entrepreneurs and their state supporters built modernity's first black majority Atlantic society. […] While it was deemed 'a place worse than hell' for Africans, the English branded it 'the richest little spot on earth'.

The introduction of sugar plantations to the West Indies in the 1640s transformed the economies of many of the islands, including Barbados. Sugar had become a staple, rather than a luxury, and was in huge demand in Europe. Sugar cane was introduced into Barbados in 1642 and by the 1650s Barbados was exporting 8,000 tons of sugar a year to England, with a value of over three million pounds. Barbados had become so financially powerful that VS Naipaul recounts a citizen of Barbados contemptuously writing in 1669 of 'a place much cried up of late, taken from the Dutch, called New York'. The contempt was justified, given that Barbados was already exporting to England nearly as much as all the American colonies combined.

As cultivation of sugar was more labour intensive than cotton or tobacco, the planters had to import workers in huge numbers. Thousands of whites came from England, Scotland and Ireland, many of whom were convicted murderers whom Cromwell had pardoned on the condition that they left the British Isles. Others were forcibly shipped away by Cromwell because they had displeased the British government on religious or political grounds. Each worker was promised a plot of land at the end of their indenture but, as it was not in the interests of the planters for the workers to survive their indentures, they often received brutal treatment.

Their treatment, however, did not compare to the inhumane and insufferable treatment that was meted out to those who soon followed: the black African slaves who were transported to Barbados in numbers of roughly two-thousand per year. Treated no better than beasts of burden, the African slaves toiled mercilessly in oppressive heat from dawn to dusk. By 1660 the white population of Barbados had, for the first time, fallen below that of the black population. Between 1660 and 1807, British ships engaging in the barbaric slave trade carried over three million African slaves to America and the Caribbean to work the land.

> Every time I hear the crack of a whip
> My blood runs cold
> I remember on the slave ship

> How they brutalize your very soul…
> O God, have mercy on our souls
>
> *'Slave Driver' – Robert Nesta Marley*

West Indian author Christopher Nicole quoted one of the slaving captains of the time as stating that his captives 'have a more dreadful apprehension of Barbados than we can have of hell, for it was the Africans' conception that Barbados floated precariously on the surface of the ocean'. 'The suicide rate in a slave coffle was every bit as high as amongst the over-strained nervous systems of the modern welfare state', wrote Nicole.

As early as 1680, when its first population census was taken, Barbados was classified as the financial capital of England's America and it would not be long before Barbados was considered the jewel in the English crown. It was the richest spot in the New World and boasted a population the equal of Boston and New York. Barbados was of such importance to England that its capital Bridgetown is one of the cities named in Tristram Hunt's *Ten Cities that Made an Empire*.

By 1700 Barbados was the chief settlement of the sugar islands and in the first twenty years of the eighteenth century the values of its annual sugar exports doubled. In the three years from 1715 to 1717, Barbados and Jamaica each exported to England produce to a value approximately as great as the exports of all the North American colonies.

Hunt believes that the returns to England from the slavery and sugar trades were so crucial that they funded the acceleration of the British Empire, the beginnings of the Industrial Revolution and the expansion of the Royal Navy. 'The history of Barbados is by no means barren of events which have materially affected the British Empire', wrote RH Schomburgk:

> If the navigation laws led to England's supremacy on the seas, that small island was the cause which led to the navigation laws. But this is not the only point of importance attached to its history;

it was here and in St Christopher's that England founded its first colonies in the southern part of America; it was here that the first sugar cane was planted upon the soil of the British dominions; it was here that many of those attached to the Royal cause sought and found an asylum.

With the development of a regional sugar and slave economy across the West Indies, Barbados exploited its position as the easternmost Caribbean island and became the hub for market intelligence, military news, fashion, culture and influence. Because of its geographical location, Barbados was strategically the most important island in the southern Caribbean. Whoever occupied Barbados held the key to the entire region. In the late eighteenth century, France, which already held a very strong hand in the West Indies, planned a major expansion of its empire. Having learned that Barbados was top of France's list, England shipped in a formidable fighting force to complement the local militia.

In 1800 twelve regiments were stationed in barracks at the Garrison Savannah, just outside Bridgetown. The Governor of Barbados was authorised to establish as much military infrastructure as required to defend the island, including parade grounds, barracks, hospitals and forts. The forts provided a protective cove for the Royal Navy, a home for almost three thousand British troops stationed in Barbados and a base from which to launch invasions and counter-attacks into neighbouring Caribbean islands.

Cricket had been played formally in Barbados since at least 1806 when St Anne's, the West Indies' first formal cricket club, was formed. And now Barbados was the headquarters of England's forces in the Windward and Leeward Islands. Permanent stationing of British troops at the St Anne's Garrison greatly accelerated interest in the game and cricket clubs quickly sprang up around the Garrison. The cult of cricket in Barbados had begun.

TWO

The Development of Cricket in Barbados

Barbados has had a long, glorious and symbiotic relationship with cricket. This sport, more than any other has made an indelible mark on the psyche, culture, economy and social life of Barbadians.

Freundel J Stuart, QC, Prime Minister of Barbados

Barbados is something of a phenomenon in the world of cricket. No more than 166 square miles in area, with great expanses of waving sugar cane, the sheer power that the game exerts among the populace has made the island cricket's richest corner of the world. In no comparable geographical space have so many great players been produced [...] Nowhere is there a more *concentrated* area of cricket enthusiasm and skill.

EW Swanton

West Indian academic and writer Keith Sandiford wrote that cricket is the one area in which Barbados has held its own against the mightiest of neighbours and that cricket fans and historical sociologists have marvelled at the fact that a nation occupying an area no more than 166 square miles has been capable of playing the game better than Englishmen and Australians. This phenomenon sprang from the fact that from as early as the nineteenth century, Bajans adopted cricket as their peculiar national symbol.

In 1841, the British army issued an order that cricket grounds be established in every barrack in the kingdom and British commanders in Barbados encouraged the locals to participate in cricket. During the second half of the nineteenth century British army teams regularly played against each other and against Barbadian teams, and from as early as that time cricket established itself as the main form of Bajan recreation. Even before the introduction of association football in Britain, Barbados had adopted cricket as its national symbol.

While the British army played an important part in developing and popularising cricket in Barbados, so did the sons of plantation owners who recruited plantation labourers to bowl to them in plantation yards and on pastures. The plantocracy also permitted tenants on the plantations to cut tracts into the grass fields, which were maintained for the provision of animal fodder, and develop them into cricket pitches. Planters also sponsored teams and encouraged regular competition.

In 1849, John Prettijohn, the English educated Bajan owner of Constant Plantation, made a field available for cricket matches between two clubs named 'City' and 'St Michael'. The Lodge School, Harrison College and Codrington College were playing cricket on a regular basis by 1855 and it was the sons of the plantocracy as well as the sons of rural white Barbadians who attended those institutions.

The first West Indian intercolonial cricket match was played between Barbados and British Guiana on the Garrison Savannah, in February 1865. Many businessmen closed their stores so that they, and their employees, could watch the game. By the 1870s social cricket was being played everywhere in Barbados, by a wide cross-section of the community. The secondary schools, parish churches, army regiments and most business firms in Bridgetown all promoted the game with enthusiasm. Cricket in Barbados had reached a good standard and the island was performing well against other Caribbean teams.

1877 marked the formation of the first of the clubs which would change the face of cricket in Barbados. Wanderers was an all-white club, its members all having money and position in society. This enabled the Wanderers club to acquire a ground, build a pavilion and provide Barbados with a firm foundation on which to build its cricketing future.

In 1882, Pickwick, the most famous of Bajan cricket clubs, was formed by whites who resented the exclusiveness of Wanderers. But black cricketers were still as unwelcome at Pickwick as 'non-upper-crust' whites were at Wanderers. Foster Alleyne, the owner of the pasture lands of Kensington Plantation, agreed to rent the ground to Pickwick at the nominal rental of one penny per year and the pasture was opened for practice on Boxing Day in 1882. This marked the birth of Kensington Oval, where all West Indies Tests in Barbados have been played.

In September 1891 Barbados hosted the first triangular cricket tournament, featuring its own teams as well as others from Trinidad and British Guiana. This tournament produced the first two West Indies cricketers of authentic international class, the Bajan brothers Percy and Clifford Goodman. The event was such a success that it demonstrated the need for a central body to administer cricket in Barbados, institute a regular intercolonial cup competition and select national teams.

This marked the beginning of organized cricket in Barbados, with the establishment in 1892 of the Barbados Cricket Challenge (BCC) committee, a self-appointed group drawn from the most eminent sections of the late nineteenth-century Bajan elite. The BCC committee arranged the first regular season and published the first set of rules governing organized cricket on the island. By this time Barbados was performing so well that it was almost invincible when playing at home.

1894 saw the formation of Spartan, Barbados's first club for black players. But Spartan exhibited its own level of exclusiveness, in that working-class black players were not welcome to join. And the administration of Bajan cricket still remained in the hands of the ruling class. The presidents of Wanderers, Pickwick and Spartan were all knighted gentlemen of privilege, such as the Master of the High Court of Chancery, the Chief Justice and the Attorney General. Even though Spartan was a cricket club for black players, its president in

1901 was Herbert Greaves, Attorney General and later Chief Justice.

The class system in Barbados was blurred, complicated and confused by racial differences. White cricketers were willing to play in the same competition as upper- and middle-class Spartan blacks, but they (as well as some upper- and middle-class blacks), were not willing to play in the same competition with labouring-class blacks.

To counter Spartan's exclusiveness, a group of working-class black Bajans formed the Empire Club, which was founded as a result of a young black fast-bowler named Herman Griffith being consistently denied membership of the Spartan club. Griffith had frightened so many batsmen while playing second division competition that no club in Barbados was willing to grant him membership. Griffith subsequently became the long-standing captain of Empire and the first black man to captain a club team in Barbados.

Bajan cricket and English cricket differed in one important area. Whereas working-class professional cricketers were the backbone of English county and Test sides, Bajan professional cricketers in the late nineteenth century were barred from participation in the BCC competition. These professionals were young men employed as groundsmen at clubs playing in the BCC competition. They had acquired reputations as skilled cricketers and were occasionally hired by clubs to play in friendly games, in order to assist club players in sharpening their own skills. But the professionals were barred from competition because they were black labourers.

Despite the limited opportunities for match play, the poor ground facilities and the scarceness of even poor quality cricket gear, the young professionals were often able to beat the best equipped clubs. Wanderers, Pickwick and Spartan played friendly matches against a team of professionals named Fenwicks, which regularly beat those three leading clubs. In spite of the racism and division amongst classes and colours, cricket flourished in Barbados and the various clubs catered to the needs of specific constituencies. Pickwick and Wanderers admitted the white and wealthy, Spartan spoke for middle-class blacks and Empire for the black working class. Such racial class distinctions actually sharpened the competitive edge, so that cricket matches became integral features of the quest for respectability and identity.

By the turn of the twentieth century Barbados was so strong that, despite its size, it was one of the 'big four' (along with Jamaica, Guyana and Trinidad and Tobago) which dominated West Indian cricket. Accordingly, Barbados was entitled to have a quota of four or more players when West Indies teams were selected for overseas tours. When the West Indies toured England in 1906, and were accorded first-class status there for the first time, Bajans accounted for half of the squad.

The star of that touring team was Bajan opening batsman George Challenor, who scored 1,000 runs for the West Indies that summer and scored his maiden first-class century against Nottingham, greatly impressing WG Grace. In 1920, batting for Wanderers, Challenor scored 261, 206 and 133 in successive innings against Pickwick and was considered to be one of the finest batsmen in the world. Challenor became the role model for several generations of West Indian players and was the first West Indian to score 5,000 first-class runs.

The West Indies team which toured England in 1923 contained five Bajans, including Percy 'Tim' Tarilton, Challenor's opening partner and the most consistent opening batsmen in the West Indies from 1905 to 1930. Tarilton set a record of 1,885 first-class runs at an average of 53.85 for Barbados and scored the first triple-century in the regional competition. He combined with George Challenor for twenty years to form the greatest pair of Bajan opening batsmen, until the appearance of Gordon Greenidge and Desmond Haynes in the late 1970s.

Challenor reached his peak during the 1923 tour, when he scored 1,556 runs at an average of 51.86, and his batting was a major factor in the West Indies being granted Test match status in 1928. Seven Bajans were in the squad on the 1928 tour to England and four were selected for the West Indies' first ever Test, at Lord's. During that Test two Bajans had the distinction of performing Test match 'firsts': George Francis bowled the first Test ball for the West Indies and George Challenor scored the first Test run.

In the early 1930s the finances of the BCC were so precarious that the merchants and wealthy planters, who subscribed substantially whenever a Bajan team went on tour, were urging the formation of a controlling association which would embrace a wider cross-section of the community. In December 1933, the Barbados Cricket Association (BCA) was incorporated by an Act of Parliament as a successor to the BCC, and the rigid social classification in Barbados cricket began to change. Under the BCA, cricket expanded at a rapid rate and Barbados was on the verge of being the cricket capital of the world.

The era of acute depression from the late 1930s to the end of the Second World War witnessed the emergence of a new generation of black cricketers who were determined to make their mark, in the same way that young black leaders were in journalism and politics. One of them was Derek Sealy, a Bajan child prodigy who in 1930 scored 58 on his Test debut as a seventeen-year-old schoolboy — still the youngest cricketer to represent the West Indies in a Test match. After his retirement Sealy taught at his alma mater, Combermere, where he coached the promising young Frank Worrell.

In 1937 'Mitchie' Hewitt organized the Barbados Cricket League (BCL), with the intention of providing opportunities for underprivileged blacks to participate in organized cricket. The BCL took competitive cricket to all the parishes of Barbados and effectively made it the national game. The League became responsible for roughly 100 clubs in the town and country divisions and was effectively the Association's nursery, producing cricketers such as Hunte, Weekes, De Peiaza, Nurse and Griffith. The establishment of the League meant that few promising young cricketers were overlooked as they moved through the divisions of the League. Hunte and Nurse were both selected to represent Barbados while still playing League cricket.

The gap in standard between English and West Indies cricket closed during the Second World War. While first-class cricket was forced to a standstill in England, Barbados and Trinidad arranged a series of Goodwill Tournaments, which produced more first-class cricket in the West Indies than the region had seen before. The result was the emergence of a number of young stars, including Bajans Weekes, Worrell, Walcott and Goddard, who would form the nucleus of West Indies Test teams for more than a decade after the war.

The 1940s were stellar years for the BCL. Fast bowler Orman Graham was selected to play for Barbados in 1943, followed by Edmund Greene and Everton Weekes, both of whom were members of the Garrison Sports Club (the Barbados Volunteer Force), which won the First Division Cup in 1947 with a team that included eight BCL players. In 1948 Weekes became the first BCL player to be selected in the West Indies Test team. Such was the success of the BCL that an annual BCA/BCL match became a fixture in the BCA's calendar until 1970.

Sir Garfield Sobers recalls that when he started playing cricket in Barbados in the early 1950s, the games between the BCL XI and the BCA XI gave many black players a chance they would not otherwise have had. Sir Garfield spoke of the strength of club cricket in Barbados at that time:

> Cricket in those days was phenomenal [...] I used to watch and score at the Wanderers ground and I was very fortunate, because the scoreboard had a kind of platform which I used to stand up on and when Spartan and Wanderers or Empire or Pickwick played there were big crowds. I had an opportunity to watch players like Everton (Weekes), Frank (Worrell), Clyde (Walcott), George Carew and all of those players that were playing for the West Indies. Also Denis Atkinson, Roy Marshall and Norman Marshall. I learned my game that way. Cricket was of a very, very high standard in those days. Barbados teams in those days certainly would have been superior to a West Indies team in the last ten, twelve years.

Along with groundbreaking developments in the political sphere came the domination of Bajan cricket by blacks. When universal adult suffrage was introduced to Barbados in 1950, the new electorate began to support black candidates. The result was that the Barbadian Legislature, which had previously been predominantly white, became predominantly black. As a result, Bajan cricket had no choice but to revolutionize. By the 1960s, cricket clubs ceased to represent separate strata of society and the white minority withdrew from politics and cricket. The vibrant new clubs which emerged were primarily black.

Today there are 128 teams participating in the BCA's competitions and on some Saturdays there are more than 200 BCA and BCL games taking place in an island that is one of the smallest cricket centres in the world. Barbados boasts an average of more than one cricket club per square mile, which helps to explain why Barbadian cricketers have been so successful as cricket professionals in Australia, England and South Africa and why the Bajan contingent has traditionally been the major element in West Indies Test teams.

> No words can adequately express the importance of cricket in Bajan culture. It surpasses all else as recreation, spectator sport, social platform and generator of national and regional pride. Wherever you go on the island at the weekend you will see serious matches being played at the many designated grounds and friendly games in full flow on the beaches. There are eighty official cricket clubs in Barbados and the game even permeates my local bank, where the sign on the closed counter does not say 'next window please' but 'next wicket please'. The eight-page sports sections of the local newspapers often lead with four pages of cricket coverage while all other sports are crammed into the remainder.
>
> *Julian Armfield*
>
> My dear Frank, I have nothing to write except that I perpetually wonder that a little scrap of West Indian territory has produced Garfield Sobers and you...
>
> *CLR James, in a 1963 letter to Frank Worrell*

Sandiford labelled this phenomenal output of talented cricketers, by such a small community occupying such a small area of the globe, a 'curiosity of modern sociology'. Cricket was favoured above all other physical exercises by the academic, political, economic and religious institutions, resulting in the whole Bajan sense of nationalism being intertwined with the game.

Barbados sends representatives to the summer Olympic Games to compete under its own flag, but does not field its own team to play Test cricket. The individual countries and territories of the Caribbean amalgamate to play under the banner of the West Indies and Barbados has produced some of the very best cricketers to have played under that banner. But, curiously, Barbados has not had great success in other sporting fields. The Barbados men's basketball team, one of the strongest teams in the Caribbean Basketball Championship, has won just four medals. The Barbados men's soccer team has never qualified for a major international tournament, making the semi-finals of the 2002 World Cup qualifiers but losing its five remaining games.

Barbados has competed in fifteen Commonwealth Games, winning eleven medals, but suffered a twenty-eight-year medal drought between 1970 and 1998. Barbadian performances at the summer Olympic Games are even more perplexing. Whereas Jamaica has won seventy-eight Olympic medals and Trinidad and Tobago have won nineteen, Barbados has won only one Olympic medal in its own right — the bronze medal won by Obadele Thompson at the Sydney 2000 Games. Bajan runner Jim Wedderburn won a medal at the 1960 Rome Games, but was running as a member of the British West Indian Federation relay team.

Barbados has more regional first-class cricket titles than any other country in the Caribbean and cricket has given the island a sense of national identity. Sandiford, in describing the story of Bajan cricket as an 'epic', claims that Barbados could have challenged any cricketing nation on even terms for decades after the Second World War, a boast few other communities could make. The New South Wales Sheffield Shield side of the 1950s was so strong that it would probably have performed well against England, or a combination of the other Australian states. And in that same decade the Surrey

County Cricket Club could probably have done the same. But neither of those teams remained as consistently powerful for as long as Barbados.

> In English terms it [Barbados] has roughly the population of Coventry, just as in size it compares with the Isle of Wight. Yet in terms of cricket it looms like a giant, its players giving both the backbone and the inspiration to one generation of the West Indies teams after another.
>
> *EW Swanton*

Barbados is smaller in land area than almost ninety-five percent of the world's countries. It is nine times smaller than Rhode Island, the smallest American state, and twenty-five times smaller than Jamaica. Compared with other cricketing nations, Barbados is minuscule. England is three hundred times larger than Barbados and India over seven thousand times larger.

By population, Barbados is ranked in the bottom two percent of the world's countries. In comparison with other Caribbean nations, it has under half the population of Guyana, a third of the population of Trinidad and Tobago and one-seventh of the population of Jamaica. Compared with Test-playing nations outside the Caribbean, Australia has forty times the population of Barbados and England one hundred and seventy-eight times the population. The cities of Pittsburgh and Nottingham have populations roughly the same as Barbados and the population of New Orleans is larger. If Barbados were a North American city, it would not rank in the top fifty US cities by population.

Yet, if measured by cricketing triumphs and the production of world-class cricketers, Barbados outstrips all other nations. In the 1950s Barbados produced twenty Test cricketers (one Test cricketer per approximately 11,000 head of population); more per capita than any other Caribbean nation or Test-playing country. In the same period Guyana produced one Test cricketer per 45,000 head of population. Trinidad and Tobago produced one Test cricketer per

66,000 citizens, and Jamaica one per 93,000. Australia produced one Test cricketer per 206,000 citizens, England one per 512,000 and India one per 6 million.

In the 1950s Barbados produced, per capita, four times more Test cricketers than Guyana, six times more than Trinidad and Tobago, eight times more than Jamaica, eighteen times more than Australia, forty-five times more than England and five hundred and fifty-seven times more than India. Compared with other cricketing nations in the 1950s and 1960s, Barbados punched well and truly above its weight.

THREE

The 'W Formation'

Everton Weekes [...] Frank Worrell [...] and Clyde Walcott were the brilliant Bajan triptych in the West Indian side that played such exciting cricket after the Second World War [...] The Ws had been born within a few-dollars-on-the-meter Bridgetown taxi fare of each other between the middle of 1924 and the end of 1926. They were a holy trinity, three consubstantial persons in one almighty side.

Simon Lister

You talk about my legacy but I prefer to look at the legacy of the Three Ws. They have left a heritage, which is our touchstone, our identity, our reference point [...] The Three Ws have established that. What we who follow should do is concretize that. Tradition is a circle that has no end, so we have to pass it on.

Wesley Hall

Many cricket historians, most notably CLR James, thought Bajan batsman George Challenor to be integral to the development of West Indian cricket. During his time in England as a youth, Challenor learnt the methods of the great batsmen of cricket's 'golden age' and brought them back to Barbados. After Challenor scored 220 against Trinidad in 1927 Bajan batsmen copied his aggressive stroke-play, which became the dominant mode for West

Indies batsmen. But he was already forty years old by the time the West Indies played its first Test series in 1928.

James and Frank Worrell were deep thinkers on cricket. Both were possessed of great knowledge of the game's history and tactics and they usually saw eye to eye. But they disagreed fundamentally on Challenor's importance to Bajan cricket. In 1963 Worrell scathingly wrote:

> One still hears of the 'scintillating' performances of the late George Challenor whose Test record I gather was an aggregate of 101 runs, highest score 46, average 16.8, but there is an ever-ready willingness to dismiss and discredit Everton Weekes's contribution of 4,455 runs, average 58.6, and Clyde Walcott's 3,796 runs, average 56.6. Weekes and Walcott have established themselves and the West Indies internationally. Could this be a case of a cricketer without honour in his own country? What is the future of a country without heroes?

Of course, Worrell was too humble to include himself in that equation, but he too played a major role in establishing the West Indies internationally, scoring 3,860 Test runs at an average of 49.48.

Worrell's assessment of Challenor was perhaps a little harsh, given that Challenor was born in 1888 and the West Indies did not play their first Test match until 1928. Although Challenor was an automatic choice for the 1928 tour to England, he turned forty that year and was well past his prime. Challenor's first-class figures are a better reflection of his skill. He played ninety-five first-class matches, scoring 5,822 runs at an average of 38.55, including 15 centuries and 29 half-centuries, with a top score of 237 not out. He also took 54 wickets at an average of 23.88. But it does not take an exhaustive study of Bajan cricket history to interpret the meaning behind Worrell's comment. George Challenor was a white man from the plantocracy, while Clyde Walcott and Everton Weekes were black men of humble origin. Worrell was, understandably, driving home the point that racial snobbishness and class distinction were alive and kicking in Barbados in the early 1960s.

Bajan writer Grantley E Edwards addressed the issue of social class in Barbados in his book *Return to Glory* and assessed the Bajan social class structure to be a crude copy of the British system. The schools cricketers attended largely determined their class and this was a criterion for club selection — attending Lodge or Harrison College marked a person as middle or upper-class, which meant they merited selection in the Barbados team. Only one of the nine premier clubs, Empire, accepted working-class cricketers.

Race played a large part in selection, as almost all the prestigious clubs were white. Race was so important at that time that the George Challenor Stand at Kensington Oval was reserved for whites. Given this social class and racial structure, it was no surprise that the captain of the Barbados team had to be white. It was not until 1960 that Everton Weekes was appointed as the first African-Bajan captain of Barbados.

In 1963 Frank Worrell wrote that one exceptional feature about Barbados was that it was the only territory in the world without a local hero. But, by the close of the 1960s, Everton Weekes, Clyde Walcott and Frank Worrell, coined 'The W Formation' or 'The Three Ws', were well and truly acknowledged as Bajan and West Indies heroes. Simon Lister relates a humorous story of the Archbishop of Canterbury visiting Bridgetown in 1969 to preach to the Anglican flock gathered in St Michael's Cathedral. When he began by saying he had come to talk about the Three Ws a huge cheer went up. But it turned into a collective groan when he continued, "Yes, the Three Ws: work, witness and worship!"

By the mid-1970s West Indian champions such as Clive Lloyd, Vivian Richards and Gordon Greenidge spoke of the impact and influence that Weekes, Walcott and Worrell had on the lives and careers of modern West Indian cricketers. The Three Ws had become household names, spoken of in the same reverential terms as Sir Jack Hobbs, Sir Donald Bradman and Walter Hammond, and acknowledged not only by Bajans but the rest of the world as three of the greatest players ever to have graced Test cricket.

By the closing decade of the twentieth century writers such as Sandiford were acknowledging that Barbados's heroes were cricketers and that cricket triumphs were the crux and essence of Bajan legend. Bajan cricket meant attractive and stylish stroke-play and Bajans had a fetish for class, beauty and elegance, preferring to be mesmerized by the manner in which a batsman plays his shots rather than be overwhelmed by a torrent of runs. The story of the W Formation is proof of that Bajan love of style and class.

In the second decade of the twenty-first century, Weekes, Worrell and Walcott are still the most famous batting combination in West Indies cricket history. They are acknowledged as one of the greatest middle-order batting combinations from any nation and their feats are still spoken of in awe in every country in which cricket is played. They scored a total of 12,113 Test runs, at a combined average of 54.8. In first-class cricket they scored a total of almost 39,000 runs at a combined average of better than 55, including 115 centuries. Weekes, Walcott and Worrell were the pillar of West Indian batting for a quarter of century, serving as role models and being idolized by thousands of youths the world over who attempted to emulate their styles and mannerisms.

The English press coined the nickname The Three Ws in April 1950, upon the arrival of the West Indies team in England. Clyde Walcott said that at the start of the tour he was not sure he deserved to be bracketed with Weekes and Worrell, as they had scored many more runs and had scored them well by anybody's standards. Nevertheless, he considered the nickname to be something of a responsibility. They had all been bracketed together and the onus was upon him not to let the other two down. Playing up to their lofty standards would require quite an effort.

The story of The Three Ws is unique. Only eighteen months separated them in age (Worrell was born first, in August 1924, and Walcott last, in January 1926) and Clyde Walcott believed that they were all delivered by the same midwife. All three were born within walking distance of each other, a few hundred yards from Kensington Oval: Worrell at Bank Hall, Walcott on Westbury

Road, and Weekes at Pickwick Gap. They made their Test debuts within three weeks of each other: Walcott and Weekes on 21 January 1948 (the first Test played by the West Indies after the end of the Second World War) and Worrell on 11 February 1948. They all played Lancashire League cricket in England around the same time: Worrell with Radcliffe from 1948, Weekes for Bacup from 1949 and Walcott for Enfield between 1951 and 1954. All three were knighted for their services to cricket: Worrell in 1964, Walcott in 1994 and Weekes in 1995. And Everton Weekes recounted in later years that they were always close friends and never rivals.

At the age of twenty-three, shortly before his Test career began, Frank Worrell left Barbados to live in Jamaica. His prodigious batting skills surfaced at a very young age, while he was living in Barbados, and he played six years of First Class cricket for Barbados before leaving for Jamaica. Worrell made his debut for Barbados at the age of eighteen and scored a triple-century (308 not out) at the age of nineteen, the youngest player to ever score a triple-century in first-class cricket. He was involved in two batting partnerships of over 500 runs while playing for Barbados; the first at the age of nineteen, when he shared a stand of 502 with John Goddard and the second at the age of twenty-one, when he partnered Clyde Walcott in a stand of 574. Worrell lived in Jamaica for most of the twenty years prior to his death, but his cricketing skills had been well and truly established in Barbados.

Weekes, Walcott and Worrell played the first of their 29 Tests together in February 1948 and the last in August 1957, a period of nine and a half years, scoring a total of 7,047 runs in those Tests at a combined average of 49.7. On the few occasions that any other Test side could boast three genuinely world-class batsmen, they did not play together for as long as the Three Ws.

The English middle-order of Denis Compton, Tom Graveney and Peter May played together for six years between 1951 and 1957. Then Graveney, May and Colin Cowdrey played together for six years between 1955 and 1961. In the same period, the top three Australian batsmen, Arthur Morris, Lindsay Hassett and Neil Harvey played together for five and a half years, between January 1948 and August 1953. Australia had an extraordinarily strong Test batting line-up in the five seasons between 1930 and 1934, when the middle-order that followed Bill Ponsford and Bill Woodfull comprised Don Bradman, Stan McCabe and Alan Kippax. But none of those successful batting combinations came close to lasting as long as the Three Ws. As Wisden stated (politically incorrectly by today's standards), 'The three coloured players from the tiny island of Barbados, Weekes, Worrell and Walcott, stood out in a class of their own.'

West Indian author and barrister Ernest Eytle described the Three Ws as a 'trinity of classic batsmanship' that combined skill, power and grace in a measure few teams have been able to match; each in his own way bringing something rich and exciting to the art of batting. Walcott, tall, heavily built yet sprightly, kept wicket with the agility of a much lighter man, then took his turn with the bat and became a punishing batsman who terrified bowlers and fieldsmen with the sheer power of his driving. He was a devastating batsman who hit the ball with a ferocity seldom equalled. Weekes, short, stocky and broad-shouldered, surprised the greatest bowlers with his crisp hooks and cuts and the great concentration that helped him pile up huge totals. Cleanly and savagely efficient in his cutting and hooking, Weekes was a neat and compact destroyer of all bowling. Worrell, lithe and graceful, stroked the ball with perfect timing. A man for the big occasion, he batted with artistry and flowing style.

One attitude the Three Ws shared was that a batsman should never use his pads to play the ball. Clyde Walcott considered that the use of the pad by batsmen, a trait developed by English batsmen in the 1950s, was a retrograde step which harmed the game. He believed that batsmen should follow the advice given by Everton Weekes when coaching youngsters: obey your instincts and use your feet to get to the pitch of the ball. It was that attitude towards the game that prompted Grantley Edwards to state that Worrell, Weekes and Walcott were pivotal in creating a brand of cricket peculiar to Barbados and the West Indies, one comprised of both science and art; a form of cricket based on attacking stroke-play combined with style and elegance.

All three of the Ws were capable of prolific scoring at the highest level. Each scored an unbeaten triple-century at first-class level: Worrell 308 not out for Barbados against Trinidad in the 1943/44 season; Walcott 314 not out, also for Barbados against Trinidad, in the 1945/46 season; and Weekes 304 not out for the West Indies against Cambridge University, in 1950. And the highest Test score for each was a double-century: Worrell 261, Walcott 220 and Weekes 207.

Former West Indies captain Jeff Stollmeyer once recalled that the inevitable question he would be asked was, "Who was the better batsman, Weekes or Worrell?" Stollmeyer believed that there were differences invisible to the casual observer, known only to their close friends and associates, and that the answer would depend entirely on existing playing conditions. He considered Worrell the sounder in defence, Weekes the greater attacking force; Worrell the more graceful, Weekes the more devastating; Worrell the more effective on soft wickets, Weekes the more so on hard wickets. Worrell gave the bowler less to work on, while Weekes had the wider range of strokes. Both were good starters, but Weekes was the more businesslike. Worrell appeared to be enjoying an afternoon's sport, whereas Weekes was 'on the job' six hours a day. Weekes took more chances than Worrell and Worrell was probably sounder overall. But Worrell was not as capable a runner as Weekes, nor was he as meticulous over the small accessories that make the complete batsman.

Clyde Walcott enjoyed batting with both Worrell and Weekes, for different reasons. He felt that Worrell's mastery made it easy for anyone to bat with him, but Weekes helped Walcott to score more quickly because the necessity to place a fielder square of the wicket to stop Weekes playing square cuts meant there was usually a gap for Walcott to play his preferred drives, if the captain neglected to change the field.

Stollmeyer wrote that both Worrell and Weekes were characters on and off the field, cheerful and humorous, and both were match-winning cricketers. In the gully or at short leg Worrell took many brilliant catches which, together with his quickness of eye and footwork, were indicative of quick reflexes. He was the complete cricketer. Weekes was a natural cricketer with a shrewd cricketing brain. One of the world's finest slip fielders, he made difficult catches appear simple.

The tables in the Appendices compare the total number of Test runs scored by the Three Ws during the period in which they all played together, with the total number of Test runs scored by the top three English and Australian batsmen during the same period. The brief summary of those tables is that between 1948 and 1958 the top three English run-scorers, Len Hutton, Denis Compton and Peter May, scored a total of 12,277 runs in the 92 Tests in which they played together, at an average of 133.4 runs per Test. The top three Australian run-scorers, Neil Harvey, Arthur Morris and Lindsay Hassett, scored a total of 10,006 runs in the 62 Tests in which they played together, at an average of 161.4 runs per Test. In the same period Weekes, Worrell and Walcott scored a total of 10,860 runs in the 54 Tests in which they played together, at an average of 201.1 runs per Test. The Three Ws averaged almost 40 more runs per Test than the top three Australians and almost 68 more runs per Test than the top three Englishmen.

In four of the six years between 1950 and 1955, the Three Ws had the highest combined batting average per Test match. In three of those years (1953–1955) Weekes, Walcott and Worrell averaged over 300 runs per Test match between them, a feat which was never achieved by the top three Englishmen or the top three Australians between 1948 and 1958. It was during those years that West Indies cricket came of age, when they beat England in England for the first time. And it was this generation of cricketers that mentored players such as Sobers, Hunte and Nurse. Worrell, Weekes and Walcott were not only the founding fathers of modern Barbados and West Indian cricket, but were also pivotal in developing modern world cricket.

Of the top ten middle-order batsmen from all Test-playing

countries who scored 1,000 or more Test runs during the 1950s, positions one, two, three and six (in terms of batting average) were occupied by Bajans. Garry Sobers in first position scored 1,115 runs at an average of 61.9. Clyde Walcott, second, scored 3,639 runs at an average of 61.7. Everton Weekes in third position scored 4,235 runs at an average of 58. And Frank Worrell, sixth, scored 2,302 runs at an average of 54.01.

Of the Test batsmen across all eras who have scored at least 2,000 runs batting in the number four position, only South African Jacques Kallis (65.2) has a higher average than Everton Weekes' average of 63.6. In third place is Australian Greg Chappell, whose average of 59.1 is four runs less per innings than that of Weekes.

The Three Ws broke the long-standing racial barrier of a sport that was held as a badge of excellence by the islands of the cricketing Caribbean. In 1956 Clyde Walcott was appointed the first black captain of British Guiana. Frank Worrell became the first permanently appointed black captain of the West Indies, in 1960. And in the same year Everton Weekes was appointed the first black captain of Barbados. Each was an unqualified success as captain.

In 1983, the Lord's Taverners asked former Test cricketers Trevor Bailey, Richie Benaud, Colin Cowdrey and Jim Laker to select their fifty greatest cricketers since the Second World War. The selection criteria were quality and excellence of performance, rather than quantity of runs or wickets. Walcott, Weekes and Worrell were all selected and the selectors had this to say of them:

> The odds against three of the world's greatest cricketers being born within a mile and eighteen months of each other on a small Caribbean island are high enough. That they should also share the same initial and follow one another in the batting order almost defies speculation [...] The Three Ws: this remarkable trio from Barbados were unquestionably the finest three, four and five in any Test team.

FOUR

The 1950s – A Great Decade For Bajan Batsmen

> Even if you were not a West Indian supporter, the 1950 series had been a great one. There had been epic batting, great bowling and, most important, cricket played at the highest level with the infectious enthusiasm that the West Indians had brought with them…The legend of Ramadhin and Valentine – and that of the Three Ws – had been born and carried them to greatness. John Goddard's captaincy had been truly magnificent…a new era had been forged.
>
> *Anton Rippon*

One of the most remarkable facts about West Indies cricket in the 1950s is that its five most dominant Test batsmen were all Bajans (Rohan Kanhai not commencing his heaviest run-scoring until the final year of the decade). Between them they plundered bowling attacks, set world records and thrilled crowds around the world. The Test batting statistics of those five Bajan batsmen during the 1950s are:

Everton Weekes: 39 Tests, 3,383 runs, average 53.7, 10 centuries, top score 207

Clyde Walcott: 35 Tests, 3,213 runs, average 59.5, 13 centuries, top score 220

Frank Worrell: 35 Tests, 2,847 runs, average 48.2, 8 centuries, top score 261

Garry Sobers: 34 Tests, 3,077 runs, average 61.5, 10 centuries, top score 365 n.o.

Conrad Hunte: 23 Tests, 1,527 runs, average 44.9, 4 centuries, top score 260

In total, they scored 14,047 Test runs at a combined average of 53.5, including 45 centuries, 8 of which were double-centuries.

The Bajan Test batting contingent was so powerful between 1948 and 1960 that in almost half of the West Indies' Test innings, Bajan batsmen scored more than 60% of the runs. In particular, the period between 1954 and 1958 was spectacular for Bajan batsmen. In almost 70% of the West Indies' innings during that period, Bajan batsmen scored more than 60% of the runs. In just over half of those innings, Bajan batsmen scored 70% or more of the runs.

Vivian Richards holds the record for the most runs scored by a West Indian batsman in a Test series (829), just shading Bajan batsman Clyde Walcott, with 827 runs, into second position. Third, fifth, eighth, ninth, eleventh and twelfth positions are occupied by Bajan batsmen, all of whom played in the second period of West Indies cricket. Garry Sobers is in third position with 824 runs. Everton Weekes occupies fifth and eighth positions, with 779 and 716 runs. Sobers and Walcott appear again in ninth and eleventh spots with 709 and 698 runs, respectively, and twelfth position is occupied by Conrad Hunte, with 622 runs.

Of the top fifty instances of most runs scored by West Indies batsmen in a Test series, twenty-one (42%) were scored by Bajans. The Caribbean country with the next highest total was Guyana, with fourteen (28%). Ten of the twenty-one Bajan instances of highest series scoring were scored in Test series played between 1948 and 1960.

Bajan Test Partnership Records from 1954–1966

West Indies Test partnership records for the 2nd, 3rd, 4th and 7th wickets were all scored between 1954 and 1960. All of the batsmen involved in those record partnerships were Bajan and all of those records stand today.

    446 for the 2nd wicket:
    3rd Test v Pakistan in Kingston, Jamaica, February 1958

Garry Sobers (365 not out) and Conrad Hunte (260) shared a world record 2nd wicket partnership of 446, the stand being broken only when Hunte was run out. This partnership was the second highest in Test cricket, falling only five runs short of the record for any wicket, being 451 by Don Bradman and Bill Ponsford for Australia against England at the Oval in 1934.

    399 for the 4th wicket:
    1st Test v England at Bridgetown, Barbados, January 1960

Sobers (226) and Frank Worrell (197 not out) shared a record 4th wicket partnership of 399, remaining together for a total of nine and a half hours and each offering only one chance. This partnership still stands as the highest West Indies 4th wicket partnership in Test cricket. It is the highest partnership for any West Indies wicket against England and the best 4th wicket stand by any country against England. Worrell batted for more than eleven hours and Sobers for just under eleven, at that time the two longest innings ever played against England.

    347 for the 7th wicket:
    4th Test v Australia at Bridgetown, Barbados, May 1955

This match was memorable for the world record 7th wicket partnership of 347 between Bajans Dennis Atkinson (219) and Clairmonte Depeiaza (122). The pair batted for more than a day. In addition, it was the maiden Test century for both batsmen.

338 for the 3rd wicket:
4th Test v England at Port of Spain, Trinidad, March 1954

Everton Weekes (206), Frank Worrell (167) and Clyde Walcott (124), all scored centuries in the same match for the first time, a batting feast Ernest Eytle described as 'a large rum punch followed by champagne and a cocktail'. The 3rd wicket stand of 338 between Weekes and Worrell was a record for any wicket in an England v West Indies series and remains the highest partnership at Port of Spain.

During the following six years, Bajan batsmen set three more West Indies Test partnership records. At Trinidad in 1962, Frank Worrell and Wes Hall shared a stand of 98 for the 10th wicket against India. At Leeds in 1966, Seymour Nurse and Garry Sobers shared a partnership of 265 for the 5th wicket against England. And at Lord's in 1966, Sobers and his cousin, David Holford, shared a stand of 274 for the 6th wicket against England. By the end of 1966, Bajan batsmen held seven of the ten West Indies' highest Test batting partnership records.

Other Bajan Batting Highlights from 1948–1958
1948–49

England toured the West Indies in the first Test series played after the end of the Second World War. Frank Worrell's batting average for the three Tests in which he played was 147.

Everton Weekes scored 141 in the final Test against England, in Jamaica. This was the start of a remarkable run. In the West Indies next match, the 1st Test against India in New Delhi, he scored 128. In the 2nd Test against India in Bombay he scored 194. In the 3rd Test in Calcutta he scored a century in each innings; a flawless 162 in the first and 101 in the second. Weekes scored four consecutive Test centuries in the series against India and five successive Test match centuries in all; a world record which still stands today.

In his next innings, the 4th Test in Madras, Weekes was run

out for 90, the victim of an umpiring decision that was described by Clyde Walcott and others who witnessed it as 'dubious'. In the first innings of the 5th Test in Bombay, in February 1949, Weekes scored 56. This meant he had also set the record for the most consecutive fifties in Test cricket; 7 between 1947 and 1949, a record which he still shares with Zimbabwe's Andy Flower. Weekes almost made it 8 fifties in a row, but was dismissed for 48 in the second innings in Bombay. Weekes' record of 7 consecutive fifties stood unchallenged for more than fifty-two years, before being equalled by Flower.

Everton Weekes scored a total of 1,350 first-class runs on the Indian tour at an average of exactly 90, including 6 centuries. In the five Tests he scored 779 runs at an average of 111.28. This is still the most runs conceded by India to any individual batsman in a Test series. Clyde Walcott scored 1,366 first-class runs on the Indian tour at an average of 75.88, including 5 centuries. In the Tests he scored 452 runs at an average of 64.57. West Indian batsmen scored 11 centuries in the Indian Tests, the second highest number of centuries by one side in a Test series, four of which were scored by Weekes and two by Walcott.

1950–51

1950 was a historic year for the West Indies Test side and for Bajan batsmen in particular. The West Indies beat England for the first time in a Test series played in England. They played 31 first-class matches on the England tour, winning 17, drawing 11 and losing only 3. West Indies batsmen scored 37 first-class centuries, 20 of which were scored by Worrell, Weekes and Walcott. Included in Weekes' 7 centuries were a triple-century and 4 double-centuries.

The West Indies had immediate success against Surrey at the Oval, when Weekes (232) and Walcott (128) shared a stand of 247, a 4th wicket record for the West Indies in England. Weekes batted for almost six hours and hit 26 fours.

Only a few days later, against Cambridge University, Weekes

(304 not out) and Worrell (160) shared a 3rd wicket stand of 350 in 225 minutes, a record for any West Indies wicket in England. Weekes batted for 325 minutes and hit 40 fours, his score being the highest individual score by a West Indian player in England and the highest score at Cambridge. Worrell batted for 270 minutes and hit 27 fours. The West Indies total of 4 for 594 declared was the highest by any West Indies team in England.

In the 1st Test against England at Old Trafford, Weekes equalled the feat of becoming the fastest batsman in Test history to reach 1,000 Test runs, sharing the record with English opening batsman Herbert Sutcliffe. Weekes achieved the feat in the 12th innings of his career, one innings fewer than Donald Bradman.

> Walcott licked them around;
> He was not out for one-hundred and sixty-eight,
> Leaving Yardley to contemplate...
>
> *'Victory Calypso' – Lord Beginner*

Clyde Walcott's score of 168 not out in the second innings of the 2nd Test at Lord's fell just one run short of the highest Test score by a West Indian player in England – George Headley's 169 in 1933. The West Indies won the Test by 326 runs, defeating England in a Test match in England for the first time. For many this was considered a defining moment, not just for West Indies cricket, but for West Indian people.

Walcott recalls that when the West Indies won the Lord's Test thousands of West Indians raced onto the field, dancing and singing the 'Victory Calypso' song. He describes the win:

> Lord's, the home and headquarters of cricket, was transformed as never before one day in late June 1950. A new atmosphere had come to Lord's. Across the time-honoured grass, with this strange slope from grandstand down to the tavern, their voices ringing from side to side swarmed a throng of my countrymen. I can hear them now, clearly as if it were yesterday. The excited

pleasure-drunk voices, the humming music of the steel percussion band; they come back to me with vivid clarity. For this was our greatest moment, the occasion for which West Indies cricket had waited and worked, hope and prayed, for so long. We had beaten England in England. And, wonder of wonders, the victory had come at the great Lord's itself [...] When we returned to our hotel the festivities went on, and we were particularly happy to be joined by a party of West Indian students. They, of course, were as excited as we were, and again came the rigmarole of explanation. "No," we told them, "not at Lord's; it was at *headquarters* we won."

Two weeks after the historic 2nd Test win, Worrell (241 not out) and Weekes (200 not out) shared a 3rd wicket stand of 340 runs in 170 minutes against Leicestershire. Weekes' first hundred was scored in sixty-five minutes, the fastest century of the English season. Worrell also shared a partnership of 247, in just over two hours, with Bajan opening batsman Roy Marshall (188). The three Bajan batsmen scored a total of 629 runs, for the loss of just one wicket.

The West Indies won the 3rd Test in Nottingham by ten wickets. Worrell (261) and Weekes (129) shared a record 4th wicket stand of 283 in the first innings. This was, at the time, the highest Test batting partnership for the West Indies for any wicket and the highest 4th wicket partnership for the West Indies in any match in England. It remains the highest 4th wicket stand in Tests at Nottingham. The West Indies' innings total of 558 was the highest total in any Test match against England.

Frank Worrell scored 239 runs in one day; the sixth highest number of runs scored in a day in Test cricket. Worrell scored 114 runs in the session between lunch and tea, one of only six players at that time to have scored a Test century between lunch and tea, and one of only two West Indian batsmen (both Bajans) to have done so. His score of 261 was the highest Test score made at Trent Bridge, until beaten by Denis Compton in 1954. It stood for twenty-six years as the highest Test score made by a West Indian in England, until Vivian Richards scored 291 at the Oval in 1976.

Wisden said of Worrell's innings:

> [He] batted in scintillating style, and the bowlers and fieldsmen were unable to check a wonderful array of fluent strokes [...] so easily did he play the bowling that there were many who considered that Worrell stood a good chance of beating Hutton's record Test score of 364.

Sir Pelham Warner, former English Test captain and *Wisden* Cricketer of the Year on two occasions, described Worrell's innings as the best batting he had seen in a lifetime of playing and watching. Michael Manley wrote of the innings:

> What Worrell displayed at Trent Bridge in 1950 was complete mastery. There is no stroke that he did not play. At the same time his cricketing intelligence was in control of everything that he did. He manoeuvred the attack to his purpose, pulling impudently across the line of spin and turn when they tried to pin him down only to crash the ball through the space created when the field was adjusted.

The West Indies won the 4th and final Test at the Oval by an innings and 56 runs. Worrell played a masterly innings, batting at three and scoring 138 despite having to leave the field at one stage suffering from exhaustion and dizziness. In the four Tests Worrell scored 539 runs at an average of 89.8, Weekes 338 runs at 56.3 and Walcott 229 runs at 45.8; a total of 1,106 Test runs for the Three Ws at a combined average of 63.9.

Weekes, Worrell and Walcott scored a total of 5,759 first-class runs on the tour at a combined average of 67.9, including 20 centuries. Weekes scored 2,310 runs at an average of 79.6, including 7 centuries and a top score of 304 not out. Worrell scored 1,775 runs, average 68.2, including 6 centuries and a top score of 261. Walcott scored 1,674 runs at an average of 55.8, including 7 centuries and a top score of 168 not out.

The West Indians returned home as heroes. The ship docked

first at Bridgetown where huge crowds, given a public holiday for the occasion, lined the streets to welcome the team home.

Clyde Walcott recalls the scene:

> When we arrived home all Barbados turned out, so it seemed, to welcome us back. Shortly before we steamed into harbour the captain of the ship received a wire to the effect that the governor of Barbados would meet us on the quay, and that there was to be a parade in our honour. The day before our arrival the harbour had been decked with flags. The scene as we came in was almost unbelievable. Crowds were swarming in every imaginable place, including the rigging of the several schooners in the harbour. All around, mingling with the enchanting sound of the steel bands, were people singing and cheering. It was a wonderful reception, which made the trip even more worthwhile for us than it had seemed.

Wisden pronounced that West Indies cricket had firmly established itself during this series, its strength being acknowledged by the fact that all future Test series played by the West Indies would be increased to five Tests. The series victory against England marked the West Indies' arrival in international cricket and was more than just a sporting success; it was proof that a people was coming of age. The West Indies had not only bested the masters at their own game, but had done so on the master's home turf.

1951–52

The West Indies toured Australia but were not able to repeat their successes of 1950, due to a number of issues. Frank Worrell was critical of the tour itinerary, which gave the West Indies only one first-class match before the first Test. There was a rift in the team regarding the question of captaincy and several players who had previously assisted captain John Goddard with advice stopped doing so. There were also injuries to key players. In the opening first-class match Everton

Weekes tore a hamstring so badly that he could not move freely for the rest of the series. Clyde Walcott broke his nose early in the series and later developed serious back trouble, which forced him to miss two Test matches and to later abandon wicket-keeping altogether.

However, there were some highlights. The West Indians struggled when they ran into bumpers for the first time in the 1st Test in Brisbane, but Weekes' second innings 70 was, by all accounts, a classic innings. While not exactly a highlight, Clyde Walcott suffered his first duck in Test cricket in this Test, but was never to suffer another. Walcott finished his career with the fewest Test match ducks among all batsmen who had played more than seventy Test innings; just one in seventy-four innings.

Frank Worrell scored a courageous 108 in the innings total of 272 in the 4th Test at Melbourne, batting for almost four hours with a swollen right hand against the pace of Lindwall and Miller. No other West Indies batsman scored more than 37 in that innings. Both Worrell and Weekes were named as *Wisden* Cricketers of the Year for 1951.

Walcott (115) and Worrell (100) shared a partnership of 189 against New Zealand in Auckland in February 1952, the highest 5th wicket partnership against New Zealand. It still stands as the record 5th wicket partnership for Tests at Auckland. Clyde Walcott scored 1,098 first-class runs on the New Zealand tour at an average of 49.9, including 4 centuries.

1953

The Three Ws punished the bowlers on the Indian tour of the West Indies. Everton Weekes produced every stroke in his repertoire to pass George Headley's 1929/30 record of 703 runs in a Test series. He scored 716 runs at an average of 102.3, including 3 centuries, which remains the highest number of runs scored in a Test series against India in the Caribbean.

In the 1st Test at Port of Spain, Weekes scored 207 in the West Indies' first innings, at that time the highest Test innings scored in

Trinidad. In doing so, he shared a record 3rd wicket stand of 338 with Frank Worrell. In the 4th Test at Georgetown, the Three Ws scored 267 of the West Indies' first innings total of 364: Walcott (125), Weekes (86) and Worrell (56).

In the 5th Test in Jamaica the Three Ws all scored centuries in the same Test innings for the first time: Worrell 237, Walcott 118 and Weekes 109. The West Indies' innings total of 576 was their highest score in a home Test and Worrell and Walcott shared a 4th wicket partnership of 213, a record for West Indies v India Tests.

Everton Weekes scored 969 first-class runs at an average of 121.1, including a top score of 253. Walcott scored 457 Test runs at an average of 76.1 and Worrell scored 398 Test runs at an average of 49.8. The Three Ws scored more than 1,500 runs in the five Tests, including six of the eight West Indies centuries.

1954

England toured the West Indies. Clyde Walcott scored 220 in the first innings of the 2nd Test in Barbados, easily outscoring England's innings total of 181 on his way to posting the highest individual Test innings scored in Barbados. Coincidentally, the West Indies won the Test by 181 runs.

In the 4th Test in Trinidad the Three Ws again all scored centuries in the same Test innings and meted out to the English bowlers one of their heaviest ever canings. Weekes scored 206, Worrell 167 and Walcott 124. Denis Atkinson also weighed in with 74, resulting in Bajan batsmen scoring a total of 571 of the West Indies' first innings total of 681. In the West Indies' second innings, Bajan batsmen scored 160 of the innings total of 212.

Everton Weekes scored 487 runs in the Tests, at an average of 69.6. During the 4th Test, he surpassed George Headley's aggregate of 2,190 runs to become the West Indies' highest Test run scorer, a record he held until June 1966 when he was surpassed by Garry Sobers. Sometimes it seemed as though Weekes was toying with the bowlers. When Brian Statham bowled to a packed offside field,

Weekes punished the ball through mid-on. When Trevor Bailey set a heavy leg-side field (as was then allowed), Weekes gave himself room outside leg stump and drove the ball through the vacant offside field. Test cricket fans in the 1980s were used to seeing Vivian Richards bat that way, but it wasn't common thirty years earlier.

1955

The Australians toured the West Indies in what proved to be a batsmen's series. Twenty-one centuries were scored and Richie Benaud described Weekes and Walcott as 'absolutely murdering' the Australian bowling attack and turning on some of the most blazing batting he had ever seen. Clyde Walcott broke three world records in the five Tests. The first was scoring 827 runs for the series, a new West Indies Test series aggregate record. The second was hitting five centuries, which remains the highest number of centuries scored by a batsman in a single Test series. And the third was becoming the first Test batsman to score a century in each innings twice in the same Test series.

In the 2nd Test in Trinidad Walcott scored a century in each innings, to become only the third West Indies batsman to achieve the feat in a Test match. In the West Indies' first innings, Weekes (139) and Walcott (126) shared a 3rd wicket partnership of 242, a record for any West Indies wicket in a Test against Australia. It stood for almost thirty years until beaten by Viv Richards and Richie Richardson in 1983/84. In the second innings Walcott (110) and Weekes (87 not out) scored almost three-quarters of the West Indies' total of 273.

Author RS Whitington recalled that this was the first time Australian fast-bowling greats Ray Lindwall and Keith Miller had come to grips with two of the 'Terrible Ws' together and in top form and that they were not accustomed to being hooked high into tamarind trees or over the top of grandstands.

The 4th Test in Barbados is memorable for the world-record 7th wicket partnership of 348 between Bajans Denis Atkinson (219) and Clairmonte Depeiaza (122). Atkinson was under pressure, as he was acting captain in place of the injured Jeff Stollmeyer and the West Indies were 6 for 146, when he was joined at the wicket by wicketkeeper Depeiaza. The pair proceeded to bat for more than a day to take the West Indies score to 510, and their record partnership still stands today.

Atkinson also became the first cricketer to score a double-century and take five wickets in an innings of the same Test match. On an unresponsive pitch, which had produced 1,661 runs, Atkinson took 5 for 56 in Australia's second innings. His feat has been equalled only once since, by Pakistan's Mushtaq Mohammad against New Zealand in 1973.

Clyde Walcott's golden series continued in the 5th Test in Jamaica. For the second time in the series, Walcott, assisted by partnerships with Weekes and Worrell, hit two separate centuries (155 and 110) in a Test match. Walcott remains the only batsman to score separate centuries in two Tests in the same series, and the only batsman to score more than four centuries in a single Test series.

1955–56

The West Indies toured New Zealand. In February 1956, Everton Weekes scored 123 at Dunedin, which was then the highest Test score at that venue. Weekes scored 418 Test runs in the series, including 3 centuries, at an average of 83.6.

1957

The West Indies did not fare well on their 1957 tour of England, both Weekes and Walcott suffering from injuries. While batting in the Edgbaston Test, Walcott suffered a leg injury so severe that he fainted at the wicket. Wes Hall recounted that Weekes was so severely plagued by sinusitis that he was vomiting in his hotel room every morning. He often went missing just before he was due to bat and would invariably be found locked in a toilet being violently ill. In addition, Weekes broke a finger in late June.

Hall was upset by journalists' accusations that Weekes and

Worrell had not attempted to get fit, explaining that the usual procedure was to leave unfit players behind in London for special treatment and rest, until they were match fit. But the decision to do so was up to management. Since that didn't happen and Weekes and Worrell were played constantly, the responsible West Indies officials must have considered them fit.

Bajan batsmen still managed to perform some heroics during the series. On the final day of the 2nd Test at Lord's, Everton Weekes scored 90 runs, despite battling the pain of a cracked bone in his right hand, while the West Indies slumped to an innings defeat. Hall recalled that Weekes' innings 'brought gasps of appreciation from the England fielders' and he considered it to be one of the most brilliant innings of Weekes' career. Sir Alec Bedser described the Lord's pitch in that Test as 'fierce' and he doubted if any batting performance ever merited higher praise. And English batting great Denis Compton considered Weekes' feat to be "in every respect, the innings of a genius'.

Frank Worrell's performance in the 3rd Test in Nottingham was one of his greatest. He bowled twenty overs in England's first innings, then opened the batting in the West Indies' first innings, after having batted at seven in the 1st Test and six in the 2nd Test. Worrell carried his bat through the innings, scoring 191 not out in 575 minutes, and he shared a record 10th wicket-stand of 55 with spinner Sonny Ramadhin. Surprisingly, Worrell did not think much of his innings, calling it far from his best. His reasoning was that bowlers got so little assistance at Trent Bridge that any batsman with a sound defence and one scoring shot could score a century.

The West Indies were forced to follow on in their second innings and Worrell and Sobers again opened. The light was so poor when they went out to bat that when England keeper Godfrey Evans enquired as to why Worrell was batting again Worrell replied, "I've come out to develop a few photographs."

Worrell was on the field from 11.30am on Thursday until 3.00pm on Monday, a total of twenty and a half hours, for what *Wisden* claims was probably the longest time any cricketer had endured. Upon coming off the ground at the end of the match Worrell's feet were so bloodied and blistered that his socks had to be prised off with hot water. That evening Worrell was unable to walk from his room to the dining room of his hotel.

Worrell again opened both the batting and bowling in the 4th Test at Leeds, taking 7 for 70 in England's first innings. He came second in the West Indies' batting averages for the series and topped the bowling averages. During the tour Everton Weekes became the first West Indies batsman to score 4,000 Test runs and only the fourth to pass 10,000 first-class runs.

1958

This year saw a continuation of Bajan batting dominance, but not by the Three Ws. In the 1st Test against Pakistan in Barbados, Conrad Hunte batted for five hours in the West Indies' first innings to score 142 in his maiden Test innings. Everton Weekes provided strong support with an innings of 197.

The 3rd Test in Kingston, Jamaica, is forever remembered for Garry Sobers' world-record score of 365 not out. Sobers scored 208 runs on the first day and batted for just over ten hours, the innings made more extraordinary by the fact that it was his maiden Test century. This score still stands as the highest maiden Test century and Sobers remains the youngest player (21 years and 216 days) to score a Test triple-century.

Sobers was given excellent support by Conrad Hunte, who scored 260 runs in their world record 2nd wicket partnership of 446, which remains the highest score for any Test partnership in Kingston. They became only the fourth pair in Test cricket to bat through a whole day's play and their stand fell only five runs short of the then world-record for all partnerships of 451 set by Don Bradman and Bill Ponsford in 1934. Hunte had scored a century and a double-century in his first two Test matches. Walcott and Weekes also scored 88 not out and 39, respectively, Bajan batsmen scoring 752 of the innings total of 790 runs. The West Indies total still stands as the highest West Indies team score and at the time was the fourth highest Test innings total.

Sobers continued his blistering form in the 4th Test in British Guiana, when he hit a century in each innings (125 and 109 not out). In the West Indies' first innings he and Clyde Walcott (145) thrashed the Pakistan attack in a brilliant 2nd wicket stand of 269. Conrad Hunte scored 114 in the West Indies' second innings, his third century in his first three Test matches. Bajan batsmen scored four centuries in the match, which the West Indies won by 8 wickets, giving them the series 3–1.

Everton Weekes scored 455 runs in the Tests at an average of 65. Clyde Walcott scored 385 runs at an average of 96.2 and was named as a *Wisden* Cricketer of the Year for 1958. But their performances were dwarfed by that of Sobers, who scored 824 Test runs at an average of 137.3, including three centuries. Sobers' aggregate remains the highest scored against Pakistan in a Test series.

Sobers scored 1,193 Test runs in the 1958 calendar year, including five centuries and a world-record highest score of 365 not out, at an average of 132.6. In little less than one year, between March 1958 and January 1959, he scored 1,115 Test runs in six successive Tests, at the incredible average of 185.8.

Between 1950 and 1966 the West Indies played in 18 Test series, of which they won 11 (61%). They played 79 Tests, winning 33 (42%), drawing 23 (29%) and losing 23 (29%). They played a higher percentage of Tests away (56%) than at home (44%) and, correspondingly, won a higher percentage of Tests away (45%) than at home (37%).

Richie Benaud and Frank Worrell

The Tied Test, Brisbane Cricket Ground, 14 December 1960
– The fall of the last wicket

The Three Ws on board the ship to England, 1950 (left to right)
– Walcott, Worrell, Weekes

Back row (left to right): W. Ferguson (scorer); A. Valentine; C. Walcott:
H. Johnson; L. Pierre; A. Rae; R. Marshall; C. Williams. Centre row (left to right):
E. Weekes; R. Christiani; J. Stollmeyer; J. Goddard (Capt.); J. Kidney (Manager);
G. Gomez; P. Jones; F. Worrell. Seated: S. Ramadhin; K. Trestrail

Crowd shot – West Indies, 1955

Everton Weekes

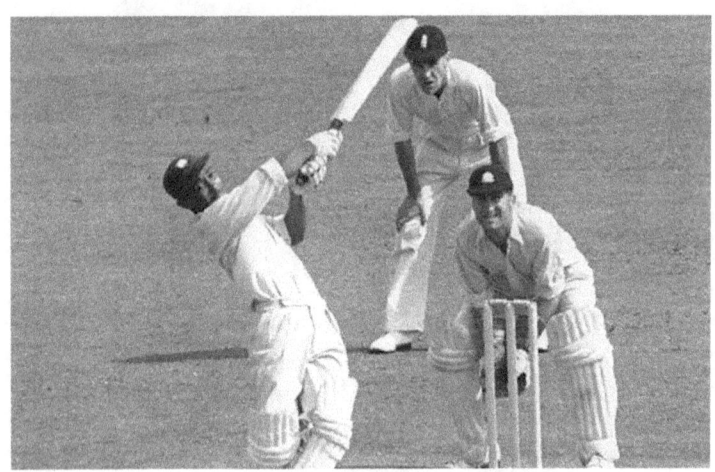

Frank Worrell

Clyde Walcott

Garfield Sobers

Wesley Hall

Barbados beach cricket at sunset

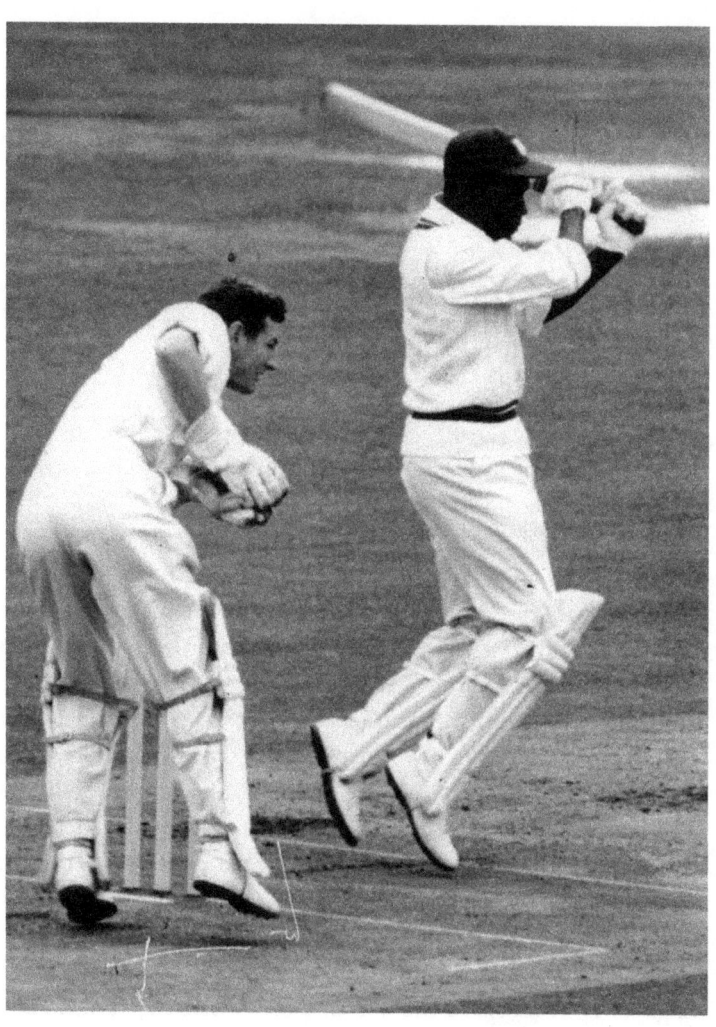

Conrad Hunte

FIVE

Why the Dominance of Bajan Test Batsmen in the 1950s?

> Per head of population, nowhere in the world has produced more and better sportsmen than this tiny strip of land.
>
> *Richie Benaud*

In the 1950s Barbados was akin to a factory for producing champion cricketers. And it wasn't as if its Test representatives in that era played only a handful of matches. Half of the Bajans who played Test cricket in the 1950s played twenty or more Tests, a higher percentage than that of any other Test-playing territory or nation. By comparison, the percentages of cricketers from other countries who played twenty or more Tests in that period were: Guyana 45%, England 41%, Australia 40%, Pakistan 38%, India 29%, Trinidad and Tobago 27%, South Africa 19%, Jamaica 18%, and New Zealand 10%.

When John Goddard led the victorious West Indies team to England in 1950, six of the sixteen tourists were Bajan, including Goddard. In 1957, seven of the seventeen West Indians whom Goddard captained in England were Bajan. On the 1951/52 tour of Australia and New Zealand, six of the seventeen tourists were Bajan.

The peak came in 1955, when eight Bajans (Weekes, Walcott, Worrell, Sobers, Denis Atkinson, Depeiaza, Frank King and Norman Marshall) were selected to play against Australia in the 3rd Test in Guyana. On that tour the Barbados side, which came close to inflicting the only loss on the Australian tourists, contained six players who had made Test centuries: Weekes, Sobers, Hunte, Atkinson, Depeiaza and Smith. As Australian writer Ken Piesse stated, "The very best teams from New South Wales and Surrey in the 1950s would have struggled to rival the might of Barbados."

West Indies batsmen scored a total of 69 single Test centuries between 1948 and 1960, 46 of which (67%) were scored by Bajan batsmen. Between 1950 and 1960 Bajan batsmen scored as many Test double-centuries as English and Australian batsmen combined. A total of 29 Test double-centuries were scored by batsmen from all countries between 1950 and 1960, the breakdown by country being the West Indies (11), England (6), Australia, South Africa and India (3 each), New Zealand (2) and Pakistan (1). Of the 11 West Indian double-centuries, 9 (82%) were scored by Bajan batsmen. Sobers, Weekes and Worrell each scored 2. Walcott, Hunte and Atkinson each scored 1.

Between 1950 and 1960 Bajan batsmen scored as many Test double-centuries as English and Australian batsmen combined. And they scored as many Test double-centuries as South African, Indian, New Zealand and Pakistan batsmen combined.

Between 1948 and 1960 there were five instances of West Indian batsmen scoring two centuries in the same Test match, four of which were by Bajan batsmen: Weekes against India in 1948/49, Walcott on two separate occasions against Australia in 1955 and Sobers against Pakistan in 1957/58.

And three of the Bajan batsmen who dominated in the 1950s still occupy spots in the top fourteen Test batting averages of all time: Everton Weekes (58.6), Garry Sobers (57.8) and Clyde Walcott (56.7).

In his book *Sixty Years on the Back Foot*, Clyde Walcott made the case that Barbados's 'equitable climate' plays a large role in the production of so many great cricketers. That is certainly one reason, but research indicates that there are a number of other factors which have contributed to cultivating such remarkable talent.

Landscape and Climate Conditions

Barbados does not fit the mould, physically, of other Caribbean islands. The main run of Caribbean islands is volcanic, being the ridges and peaks of an underwater mountain range. In contrast, Barbados has just one small area of solid rock in the northeast, which was forced upwards by a seismic clash between the Atlantic and Caribbean tectonic plates. Most of Barbados is made of coral limestone that has gradually built up to a depth of around 300 feet.

This physical feature, coupled with the fact that there is sufficient rain in Barbados to make the soil bind well, meant that excellent, well-paced cricket pitches could be prepared without much difficulty. Such good pitches aided not only fast bowlers, who could get something out of the wicket, but also batsmen, in that they could be confident of true bounce and bat attackingly.

The flatness of Barbados's pitches produced uncomplicated cricketers, who revelled in scoring as many runs as possible and bowling with all the speed they could muster. Garry Sobers wrote in *Cricket in the Sun* that Bajan cricketers just did what was natural; the only theory about cricket in Barbados was that the batsman's business was to make runs, the bowler's to get him out, and the fielders' to prevent the former and assist the latter. Added to that, he believed that Bajan cricketers had fewer distractions than they perhaps would have had elsewhere, in that Barbados had only three principal preoccupations: growing sugar, making rum and playing cricket. "Given fast, true pitches, a climate as nearly ideal as could be desired, a natural passion for the game encouraged by rich material rewards for excelling at it, and first-class organisation at the top level, the results seem inevitable," Sobers said.

The extreme pace of Bajan fast bowlers may have something to do with the fact that Barbados has only undulating hills but no mountain range, resulting in less atmosphere and movement to assist bowlers. Piesse suggests that this may have forced Bajan pace-men to bowl fast out of necessity. Also, the average temperature in Barbados is a comfortable 29–31 degrees Celsius, with little variation throughout the year. Such a climate, coupled with a low humidity due to the trade winds, makes a day in the field not too exhausting.

Clyde Walcott believed that another beneficial factor is Barbados's scores of hospitable sandy beaches, which are open to everyone. In Barbados, a sandy beach coupled with hot weather creates an ideal scenario for an impromptu cricket match to be played, almost anytime. The use of a tennis ball on wet sand aids pace and bounce, without any risk of injury to the batsman. Batsmen can get behind the ball and play their shots, the customary treatment of a bouncer being to hook it as far into the sea as possible.

Sandiford also makes a case for the effect of Barbadian climatic conditions on the skills of its batsmen. In the 1800s the Barbadian sugar plantocracy was so influential that it controlled most aspects of life, including sport. Cricket in nineteenth-century Barbados mirrored the interests and values of these elite, which was evident even in the manner in which the annual cricket seasons were arranged. In accordance with the harvesting needs of the plantocracy, the cricket season had to begin in July and end in February, which illogically coincided with the worst weather. However, in Sandiford's view this quirk in the schedule taught Bajan batsmen how to adjust to sticky pitches, thus contributing to the production of some of the world's finest batsmen from the 1890s onwards.

The 'Englishness' of Barbados

Barbados has never changed hands since the British settled in 1627, which is partly explained by its position as the most easterly of the Caribbean islands. Mounting an invasion from the east meant a long voyage across the Atlantic while attacking from the west was almost impossible, because the prevailing trade winds blow from east to west. Historian Owen Rutter wrote:

> The early colonists found no foreign tradition in their island, as the English settlers found in Trinidad and Jamaica; there were no remnants of an alien occupation to assimilate or discard, no body

of law or custom to be scrapped or adapted. Barbados was a slate on which there was nothing to rub out. No improvisation was necessary; the colonists began as they meant to go on, as they have gone on for three hundred years.

Rutter observed that although many Bajans had never set foot in England, they were 'more English than the English'. The early pioneers modelled their colony on English tradition, even erecting a statue of Lord Nelson to commemorate his pursuit of the French fleet into Carlisle Bay. West Indian historian Philip Sherlock noted that early records from Jamaica and Barbados show that English institutions were introduced into the islands in a natural way. The method of running the affairs of a parish through a vestry, developed in England by the Tudors, was transferred to the older English colonies in the Caribbean; the freeholders of the parish electing those who would levy the rates for poor relief, the upkeep of roads, payment of the clergymen and teachers and the control of vagabonds.

Twenty-first-century Bajans may find references to 'Little England' and the 'Englishness' of Barbados irritating, particularly young Bajans who have no more reason to feel connected to England or any notion of Englishness than do young Australians or New Zealanders. West Indian writer and social commentator Olutoye Walrond believes that the notion of Barbados being a little England is rooted more in fantasy than fact and British influences are no longer the only ones shaping the Bajan cultural landscape. Twenty-first-century Bridgetown has as much in common with America as it has with England; Trafalgar Square is now National Heroes Square and to many Bajans Nelson is not a hero of Barbados. Some historians maintain that although Nelson was not a slave trader, he opposed the movement to abolish slavery and was a defender of the plantocracy. Like most Commonwealth nations, Barbados has forged its own identity since attaining its independence.

However, the main era on which this book focuses is a decade or more prior to Bajan independence, which was a very different time. Hunt wrote that the Englishness of Barbados, 'its cathedrals, parliament, parishes, cricket pitches, garrisons and gardens', was a source of pride in the eighteenth and nineteenth centuries.

> [Barbados] has been ours for two centuries and three-quarters, and was organized from the first on English traditional lines, with its constitution, its parishes and parish churches and churchwardens, and schools and parsons, all on the old model; which the unprogressive inhabitants have been wise enough to leave undisturbed. On no one of our foreign possessions is the print of England's foot more strongly impressed than on Barbados.
>
> *JA Froude*

The curiosity of Barbados's Englishness continued even after the abolition of slavery. On 1 August 1834 there were 84,000 free people in Barbados, who only the day before had been slaves. Once emancipated, the former slaves looked to establish themselves in society. In Jamaica and Trinidad there was available land, which the freed slaves could either squat on or buy. But this was not the case in Barbados. Author Mary Chamberlain explains:

> Convinced that slave emancipation would sound the death knell of a ready supply of labour and that market forces would generate unacceptably high wages, Barbadian planters responded by passing the 1840 Masters and Servants Act, which tied plantation labourers to the plantation by linking employment with land rental. The structure of land ownership and occupancy in Barbados meant that there was little or no land which could be appropriated or squatted on, and plantation labourers had little choice but to comply.

This freed black population had to exploit every other possibility for survival and so sought employment as labourers. A historical report on the condition of Barbados at the time stated that as there were so many white servants and poor whites who worked in the fields, and so many blacks who had become tradesmen, there were now thousands of slaves who spoke English. Along with learning to speak English came mastering the English ways of life, which included playing cricket.

Sir Hilary Beckles thought it unsurprising that the Bajan plantocracy seemed determined to entrench cricket culture. They had already defined their island home as Little England and held steadfast to the view that they were Englishmen in a far-flung shire separated by a large sea and a few centuries. These divisive elements were insufficient to erode their cultural rights and they took pride in defining themselves as the most loyal colonial subjects of the Crown. The worship of the cricket culture was one way in which they expressed fidelity.

Sandiford refers to a Bajan 'cricketing craze', which owed much to the soldiers, priests, politicians and educators who left England in the nineteenth century with the view of civilizing the empire, and who equated the spread of civilization with the adoption of 'the three Cs': Christianity, appreciation for the Classics, and Cricket. Whereas most sports were dismissed as skylarking, cricket was viewed as the most effective socializing agent and the best means of social control; a medium through which colonists could be civilized and brought into the imperial fold.

Chamberlain explains that as the Second World War approached, England sought to further entrench the Englishness of Barbados. England had become fearful of West Indian loyalty, believing that Nazis would exploit racial tensions in order to turn the West Indies against the Allies. The Colonial Secretary believed that, in the absence of any other sources of 'authentic' information, the 'Negro section' would be the natural prey of mischievous propaganda, such as the doctrine that 'the white man's war is the black man's opportunity'.

Barbados, because of its strategic position, needed to be unequivocally on side. The governor, Sir John Waddington, began monthly broadcasts on the Experimental Broadcast Station. English propaganda, carefully tailored to suit the West Indian "mentality", included reports on the British Royal family, cricket, West Indian students in the United Kingdom and the importance of West Indian products to the war.

Village Communities

Grantley Edwards explains that Bajan village communities were based on an African concept of living and were at the heart of Barbados cricket organization. Each village fostered an identity and the cricket team was part of that identity. Villagers came out in large numbers to support their teams, which represented and expressed the will of the villages. These teams were comprised of local boys and young men who played on the beaches, on the streets and on any piece of vacant land. As boys they played all day, every day and copied their heroes. They competed fiercely, criticising batsmen who played across the line, failed to get behind the ball or lacked grace and style, and frowning upon bowlers who bowled long hops. Edwards contends that Bajans of the 1950s knew the true history and tradition of Barbados. They learned their cricket when very young at the 'village academies' across Barbados and had 'a confidence bordering on arrogance'.

The Schools of Barbados

One of the most important influences on the growth of Bajan cricket was the strong cricket culture established in Barbados's schools, from as early as the eighteenth century. This was so important to the development of Bajan cricket that Sandiford devoted an entire book, *Cricket Nurseries of Colonial Barbados,* to the subject. Bajan school headmasters helped establish the cult of cricket and transformed the three leading secondary schools (Combermere, Harrison College and the Lodge) into 'cricket factories' during the century before the attaining of Bajan independence.

From as early as the 1860s, secondary schools and churches in Barbados used cricket as a socializing and civilizing agent. In nineteenth-century Barbados the schools were dominated by headmasters who had come from a Victorian Britain steeped in the public school ethos, which placed great store on team sports. Horace Deighton, headmaster of Harrison College from 1872 to 1905, was convinced that there was no possibility of a strong mind being accompanied by a feeble body and so made cricket an integral feature of the school curriculum. He considered it to be a prime medium for learning civic virtues and was convinced that the achievements of his boys on the cricket field were a sound reflection of the physical, spiritual and mental health of their school.

These early pioneers of the cricket cult not only popularized cricket but also produced several generations of scholar-athletes who kept the cricket craze alive long after the pioneers had died. Sandiford states that for more than a century after its emergence as a first-grade secondary school in the late 1870s, Harrison College was dominated by 'muscular Christians' who continued to preach Deighton's message. They encouraged all boys to play cricket in the belief that it would make them better Christian gentlemen and loyal Bajan citizens and urged their parents to make it possible for them to do so. After leaving school these boys took cricket with them wherever they went in their adulthood and the 'cricket cult' has held the imagination of Bajans to this day, spreading from the churches and the schools to the civil service, the courts of law and business firms.

Both Frank Worrell and Clyde Walcott believed that a large contributing factor to the production of so many outstanding cricketers was the fact that leading schools in Barbados took part in First Division matches with the senior clubs. One of the great advantages young Bajan schoolboys had over their counterparts was the opportunity of playing against recognised cricketers while still at school. By the time a young player was about to leave school he may have had four years' experience in the local senior club competition, which enabled him to walk into any of the senior club sides without any readjustment or necessity for a transition period. Clyde Walcott was a perfect example, making his first-team debut in the BCA competition for Combermere School at the age of eleven; the youngest player to appear in a BCA first-team cricket.

On that subject, Frank Worrell wrote:

> In 1937 I transferred to the secondary or grammar school – Combermere School. I was there until 1943, by which time I had tasted the thrill of first-class cricket. Yes, I played first-class cricket when I was at the secondary school [...] By the end of October [1937] I was in the first eleven [...] which meant first-class cricket, for the schools take part in first-class cricket in Barbados [...] The school teams are made up of both pupils and masters, and we had on our staff Derek Sealey, who was a former West Indian Test player [...] I found myself up against some of the best players in the West Indies, and there is no better way of learning anything than by coming up against the finest exponents [...] I never regretted the fact that as an inexperienced thirteen-year-old I had to face the bowling of Manny Martindale, who had spread alarm and despondency more than once among the England batsmen [...] In 1941 our school won the 1st XI Championship, which is the Barbados equivalent of the English County Championship.

Children's Cricket

Ernest Eytle described the many novel forms of informal cricket enjoyed by Bajan youngsters, which sharpened the eye in a way that no professional coaching could. What these games lacked in orthodoxy was compensated for by a passion for hitting the ball hard, getting it away from the fielders and, above all, getting on with the game.

'Knee cricket' was played with a marble, a toy bat and one knee on the ground. If the batsman struck the marble he would get up off his knee and run to the bowler's end. But if the marble passed his bat and the wicketkeeper broke the stumps before the bat touched the ground, then the batsman was out. Eytle reported seeing knee cricket played in a dressing-room during a Test match, the adults enjoying it as much as they had when they were children.

'Firms' was a form of cricket whereby two or three players joined together as a firm. If a member of a firm took a catch then it was his turn to bat and he was entitled to give the ball to another member of his firm. Possession of the ball was the important thing, so catching was the essential key. Also, beach cricket is still hugely popular, the fielders sometimes swimming out to their fielding positions. The pitch is set close to the water and the batsman is out if caught on the full or on the first bounce off either land or sea.

Lilliput or 'hopping ball' cricket was played by Bajan youngsters using either a knitted ball rolled in tar or a tennis ball, on a small pitch. Sir Garfield Sobers believes that the joy of Lilliput cricket was that from the earliest age young players could play the ball without fear of being hurt if they were hit, the lack of fear encouraging them to hit the ball hard and often. Sobers wrote:

> The unusual position of batting on one knee, having to keep the foot firmly on the ground and the bat in the block means that the wrist, arms, shoulders and trunk all have to be used with maximum effect [...] This position is ideal for playing the hook shot and the leg sweep. Square cuts and cover drives also become well developed.

Eytle considered that these raw and improvised variations of the game nurtured cricket in Barbados. From the time boys were old enough to grip a bat they were gripped by the fever, and were happy to get a game going on any piece of land they could find and play it according to whatever rules they agreed. The effect of this carefree approach to cricket can be seen in later years when young players throw themselves into the game with the same enthusiasm they displayed on the beach or the back yard. No amount of coaching could destroy the natural zeal and skill derived from these early forms of contact with the game.

The Clubs

Barbados has a long-standing club cricket culture, boasting an average of more than one cricket club per square mile. Frank Worrell believed that the concentration of cricket clubs in Barbados was a contributory factor in the early emergence of young Bajan cricketers into intercolonial and international cricket, as the young cricketer in his day had the opportunity of walking or cycling less than three miles on any Saturday afternoon to watch as many as six matches. The significance was that young players could learn by observation and emulation from the cream of every team in the local competitions.

Club cricket assumed great importance in the early days when Test and first-class fixtures were irregular and thousands of spectators would turn out for big club matches. The scores in the 1921 Division 1 final between Pickwick and Wanderers were indicative of the standard of the day. The match took seven consecutive Saturdays to complete, Wanderers scoring 590 and 489 to Pickwick's 436 and 284; a total of 1,799 runs for the match. It is unlikely that any other community would show such total commitment to any other sport, such that it would devote the better part of seven consecutive weekends to completing a single game.

Economic Conditions

Social conditions faced by black Bajans in the 1930s were bleak. The Great Depression of the 1930s devastated the already precarious West Indies economies and the even more precarious household economies of its workers. Added to this was the problem that Barbados was already one of the poorest of Britain's Caribbean territories.

The price of sugar, on which Barbados's economy was wholly dependent, fell to an all-time low in 1934. Further, the economic crises in Cuba, Panama and the Dominican Republic triggered a backlash against West Indian migrant workers who then returned to their home countries. The sudden increase of Barbados's population had a crushing effect because levels of unemployment were already high. Most labourers could not find year-round work and wages paid to Bajan agricultural workers (one shilling per day) were the lowest in the British West Indies.

Malnutrition was rife and infant and child mortality in Barbados was the highest in the West Indies. Chamberlain records that in 1921 42% of the burials recorded were those of children under the age of five and the figure was still 41% in 1937. In 1938, infant mortality was 221 per thousand births (more than three times the rate of Trinidad and Tobago) and the highest in the Caribbean. Life expectancy in Barbados was the lowest in the West Indies: 49 for a male and 52 for a female in 1947.

These problems were compounded by racial divisions. Universal suffrage was not introduced in Barbados until 1950. Before then eligibility to vote was determined by gender and property ownership or income. Thus, it was set beyond the reach of all but the highest paid or land rich. In 1938, the voters numbered just 10% of the adult male population.

Conditions for blacks in Barbados in the 1930s and 1940s were little short of intolerable and cricket was one of the few means of temporary escape. The significance of cricket in Barbadian life at that time is evidenced by the fact that the Barbados Cricket Association was still admitting additional teams during the era of the Depression. The strength of the game was not undermined by the economic slump and new teams, such as Empire, were deliberately established to cater to those for whom there was no place in the richer clubs.

This unique combination of beneficial landscape and climatic conditions, strong English cultural influence, village living, a strong cricket culture in schools, encouragement of informal forms of cricket for youngsters, long-standing and well organized club cricket and economic conditions resulted in the cricket cult spreading throughout the whole of Bajan society.

Goodwin suggested that while cricket is undeniably important in Jamaica and Trinidad, those islands have tended to be associated as much with music as cricket. As popular as cricket has been in

Jamaica, a clutch of Reggae's elder statesmen such as Bob Marley, Peter Tosh, Bunny Wailer, Jimmy Cliff and Winston ('Burning Spear') Rodney remain its most globally recognized citizens, and the Reggae Sunsplash festivals of the 1980s attracted larger crowds than did Test matches at Sabina Park. Similarly, tourists to Trinidad and Tobago have tended to come more for carnival than cricket. Cricket has always been important in Jamaica and Trinidad, but it is only one factor in their entertainment fields.

Barbados, however, has nothing to rival cricket for attention. Its political history has been tranquil, its politics are low-key and everything is so steeped in the spirit of cricket that to promote Barbados is to promote the game. Bajan bartenders, waiters and taxi drivers have long been renowned for their knowledge of the game and are likely to be more aware of the finer points than their counterparts in some other communities, or even some professional commentators.

In Barbados, cricket metaphors and allusions form part of the language. When Test matches are being played in Barbados, it is not unusual for half-holidays to be declared in the workplace and teachers may curtail the hours of study to allow their students, and themselves, to watch Bajan cricketers play. Exciting Test matches have been known to bring business in Barbados to a standstill. No other activity has succeeded in galvanizing the country in such a way.

SIX

Frank Worrell and the 1960s

Sir Grantley Adams, Prime Minister of the defunct West Indian Federation, said that before he left Barbados he had read all the major Greek philosophers and could read Greek as easily as English...Barbados offered black men the opportunity to learn the foundations of what British civilization had to offer, but they had to go to Britain in order to express their knowledge and the principles that they had learnt. When in 1959 Frank Worrell became the first black captain of the West Indies cricket team, it was a notable climax of more than a century of social restraint and, at last, successful endeavour.

CLR James

1960 ushered in the third period of West Indies Test cricket and the appointment of Frank Worrell as captain. The West Indies had already had a black captain, but only temporarily. In 1948, Jamaican batting great George Headley was selected as the first black captain of the West Indies for the first Test against England. He batted last in the West Indies' second innings, due to a back injury suffered while fielding, the injury proving so serious that he took no further part in the series. Headley went on the 1948/49 tour to India, not as captain, but was forced to return home injured after the first Test. At the age of forty-four he was recalled for the last time to face the might of the English fast bowlers. In the Kingston Test, Headley fell cheaply to finger spinner Tony Lock, the result of a delivery Clyde Walcott described as the most blatant throw he had seen. In his short Test career Headley scored 2,135 runs at the remarkable average of 60.83, including 10 centuries.

The West Indies captaincy issue simmered for years after. West Indian author Michael Malec reported that from as early as the 1920s Learie Constantine had been a firm proponent of the West Indies being captained by a black man. In the spirit of fair play he wanted to see a West Indies team selected on merit alone. Constantine's team would be led by a captain who could motivate West Indians, meaning that the leader would have to be an Afro-West Indian.

In the 1950s, black players, writers and commentators resented the fact that no black player had ever captained the West Indies on a permanent basis and the calls for a black captain, specifically Worrell, had become increasingly strident. Worrell had been offered the captaincy for the home series against Pakistan in 1957/58 and the away series against India and Pakistan in 1958/59, but he refused it on both occasions because of his university study commitments. He finally accepted the captaincy for the West Indies tour to Australia in 1960/61, not just because of perceived pressure from journalists and the West Indian public, but also because Gerry Alexander was finding it difficult to captain and keep wickets and was quite content to play under Worrell.

It was commonly agreed that Worrell was the only practical choice as leader. James believed that Worrell's passion was to prove that West Indian Test cricketers could be as good as other Test players, and when he was appointed captain of the team he knew what he had to do and how it had to be done. It was not just Worrell's talent and knowledge of the game that were crucial, but also his temperament. His appointment as captain was the catalyst for the West Indies taking the final leap to become the dominant team in world cricket.

In 1959/60, Peter May took his English side to the West Indies. Garry Sobers had a brilliant series, scoring 709 Test runs at an average of 101.3. Although Frank Worrell missed one of the Tests through injury, he scored 320 Test runs at an average of 64. And the new Bajan fast bowler Wesley Hall took 22 Test wickets.

In the 1st Test against England in Barbados, Worrell and Sobers batted for nine and a half hours in sharing a partnership of 399 runs. Sobers scored 226 and Worrell 197 not out, each batsman offering only one chance during his innings. Worrell batted for over eleven hours and Sobers for over ten. At that time they were the two longest innings ever played against England, and Sobers and Worrell also became the first pair to bat throughout two consecutive days of a Test match. This partnership was then the highest 4th wicket stand by any country against England. It still stands as the highest West Indies fourth-wicket Test partnership in Barbados and also the West Indian record for any wicket against England.

1960/61: Tour of Australia

Worrell was now captain, and from the time the touring party landed in Perth he made it clear that his aim was to play bright, attacking cricket, whatever the results. He was of the view that if the West Indies could win a reputation for attractive cricket then they were sure to draw big crowds. Bajans Seymour Nurse and Garry Sobers showed good early form against the Western Australian side, Sobers scoring a century and Nurse 97. The West Indies were allowed the run of Perth's WACA ground for training, which Worrell put to good use by making the players work on their fielding weaknesses. Worrell instigated a rota system of giving every player a chance in the tour matches. He worked on the idea that each player selected for the tour was potentially a Test player and would be given the opportunity to show his form in matches scheduled between the Tests.

Worrell recalled after the series that one of the most pleasing aspects for him was that Richie Benaud was of the same mind as he; both captains accepted any challenge that was thrown at them and neither set a defensive field at any stage of the series.

Coupled with the batsmen of both sides wanting to be punishing and aggressive, it made for the most enjoyable series Worrell had played in.

1960: 1st Test v Australia at Brisbane

Frank Worrell's first Test as West Indies captain, the famous tied Test, could not have been more dramatic. Worrell won the toss and elected to bat. At 2/42 Sobers entered the fray and once Worrell joined him the run rate exceeded anything seen at the Brisbane Cricket Ground for years. Sobers proceeded to play one of the great Test innings. Few balls got past his bat and he seldom played a defensive stroke. Australian journalist Phil Tressider wrote that Sobers gave the Australian bowlers their most humiliating thrashing in decades in an 'orgy of blazing boundary-hitting'. The West Indies scored 455 in their first innings and at the close of the second day Australia was 4/196. The next day Norman O'Neill showed that Sobers was not the only batsman who would play the innings of his life, pulling out all the stops in scoring 181.

The Australians scored 505 to take a first innings lead of 50, but Worrell had no intention of asking his batsmen to exercise any caution in the West Indies' second innings. Alan Davidson bowled well to restrict the West Indies' total to a modest 284, leaving Australia 232 runs to win in the fourth innings.

The last innings started dramatically, Wes Hall dismissing Bob Simpson for 0 to have Australia reeling at 1/1. Soon Neil Harvey was gone and Australia was 2/7. Davidson and Ken MacKay then settled the ship for a while before MacKay was bowled by Sonny Ramadhin, leaving Australia at 6/92. Then Davidson and Richie Benaud, each scoring fifties, shared a partnership which looked as though it would take Australia to victory. But Davidson was run out by Joe Solomon and Benaud was out soon after, trying to hook Hall. With seven wickets down, the match went into the most famous final over in Test history. Benaud later reflected, "Never before have I played in a game so full of electrifying thrills, so riddled with periods of nerve-curdling strain." The result was a triumph of leadership by both Worrell and Benaud.

By playing enterprising cricket Worrell's well-disciplined team had brought Test cricket to life again, prompting former Australian Test batsman Jack Fingleton to state in *Wisden*, "In Brisbane, at a time when many were lamenting that the game was dying, cricket was never more alive in its challenge, in its brilliance, in its down-to-earth honesty."

Australian journalist Johnny Moyes, who had a keen appreciation of attacking cricket and once scored 208 runs in 83 minutes for his Sydney first-grade side, summed up the series:

> Those who had the pleasure of watching the West Indian cricketers in action and of knowing them personally will never forget them [...] They gave the genuine cricket lover a thrill he had not felt for a quarter of a century. They brought back to the grounds many who had left them in disgust at the mediocre fare served up to them [...] They left behind them from Perth to Brisbane and back again to Melbourne a trail of admirers who took them to their hearts and who will never forget them.

Frank Worrell believed that the tied Test had set the series alight and given the Australian crowds a glimpse of the type of cricket the West Indians were pledged to play. But cricket is a great leveller. In the next Test in Melbourne, only days after the incredible highs of the tied Test, Worrell achieved the unwanted distinction of being one of only fifteen batsmen in the history of Test cricket to have been dismissed for a 'pair' on the same day.

1961/62: West Indies v India in the West Indies

Under Worrell's captaincy the West Indies won all five Tests against India, a feat performed only twice before in Test cricket history by a captain in a new series of Tests. Worrell scored 332 Test runs at an average of 83. A serious incident occurred during the tour, when Indian captain Nari Contractor was hit on the head by fast bowler Charlie Griffith while batting against Barbados. He lost consciousness and when it became known that he would require blood transfusions, Frank Worrell was the chief donor. By the end of 1962, Garry Sobers had batted in 71 Test innings and scored 3,776 runs, at an average of 69, the second highest average in Test cricket, behind only Sir Donald Bradman.

1963: West Indies in England

> I think the West Indies will out-bat, out-bowl and out-field England next year, and that Garry Sobers will prove to the world that he is the finest cricketer alive today.
>
> *Everton Weekes*

The 1963 tour of England was Worrell's last Test series. The West Indies won the series 3–1 and the tour lifted Test cricket to a new level of public interest and excitement. Bajans Worrell, Hunte, Hall, Nurse, Griffith and Allan contributed heavily to the West Indies' success. And Sobers fulfilled Everton Weekes' prophecy, proving himself the world's greatest all-rounder. Bajan fast bowlers dominated this series, the Hall and Griffith combination becoming one of the most devastating new ball partnerships seen in England.

The 2nd Test at Lord's, so intriguing that it was the subject of an entire book by Alan Ross, was one of the great Test matches of the twentieth century. Frank Worrell described the fortunes as swaying to and fro before the match ended in a tense final over draw. However, it could have ended differently, Worrell revealing that it was not generally known that with twelve balls remaining Charlie Griffith yorked Derek Shackleton, but the bails did not fall off. The ball hit the base of the stump and ran down to deep fine leg, the batsmen taking a single. Griffith took 5 for 91 in England's first innings and Hall took 4 for 93 in the second. As with the tied Test three years earlier, Hall bowled his heart out and had the responsibility of bowling the tense final over.

In the 3rd Test at Leeds, Griffith took 6 for 36 in England's first innings and the West Indies won by 221 runs. In the final Test at the Oval, Griffith took 6 for 71 in England's first innings and Hall 4 for 39 in the second. The West Indies won the Test by 8 wickets and the series 3–1. The 1963 tour was the pinnacle of Charlie Griffith's career. He took 32 Test wickets in the series, at an average of only 16.21, his yorker being particularly destructive.

The 1963 tour to England had the same effect on the English public as the 1960/61 tour had on the Australian public. Worrell reflected on the fact that the series was contested in the most friendly manner of all England v West Indies series that he had experienced and there had been great camaraderie between the two teams both on and off the field. When it was realized that the West Indies were not scheduled to return to England for a Test tour until 1968, the public reaction was such that the authorities changed the schedule so that they would instead return in 1966.

At the end of the year Worrell stated:

> I have had a great run and, as I have satisfied my greatest ambition in the last two years, I have no complaints. My aim was always to see West Indies moulded from a rabble of brilliant island individuals into a real team – and I've done it.

Garry Sobers, Conrad Hunte and Charlie Griffith were named as *Wisden* Cricketers of the Year for 1964. Barbados achieved political independence in 1966, the year in which the West Indies won the Test series against England, in England, 3–1. The West Indies team which drew the 2nd Test at Lord's contained seven Bajans: Sobers, Hunte, Hall, Griffith, Nurse, Allan and Holford. In that Test the West Indies scored a match total of 638 runs, 496 of which were scored by Bajans. West Indies bowlers took a match total of fourteen wickets, ten of which were taken by Bajan bowlers. Shortly after the conclusion of the 2nd Test, James expressed the opinion that a Barbados XI could meet an all England or all Australia XI on equal terms. That was quite a call, considering that the English side in 1966 included Boycott, Edrich, Graveney and Cowdrey, and the Australian side boasted Simpson, Lawry, Walters, Cowper, Ian Chappell, Stackpole, Grout and McKenzie.

Barbados achieved its independence in November 1966 and in March 1967, as part of the independence celebrations, the Banks Brewery sponsored a cricket match in which a Barbados team would play a Rest of the World side. Many Bajans were excited about the game, but not all saw it as a reason for celebration. A white Rhodesian and a white South African had been selected in the Rest of the World squad and many Bajans, including politicians, objected to the possibility of two white southern Africans playing cricket in Barbados. Even the usually reticent Everton Weekes opposed the idea, having visited southern Rhodesia and witnessed the racism which then existed. Frank Worrell also dismissed the game as savouring of 'bigotry, vanity and insularity'. He thought that the only possible reason for the match seemed to be to permit Bajans to prove that the Barbados team was better than the West Indies team.

Tragically, only days after the conclusion of the celebration match Sir Frank Worrell died of leukaemia at just forty-two years of age. McDonald recalls that when Sir Vivian Richards and his friends were boys they played with home-made bats on which they had scrawled the names 'Worrell' and 'Sobers', and they were playing cricket on the day Frank Worrell died. Richards recalls, "Sir Frank was a West Indian hero and everyone was proud of him. He made so many great runs against England and he led his country. It was terribly sad to hear that he had died." A memorial service was held in Worrell's honour in Westminster Abbey, the first time such an honour was granted to a sportsman.

Prophetically, 1967 would mark the start of a decline in West Indies cricket. Simon Lister wrote that the best players were stale after years of cricket and had not been replaced. That weakness caused division, and the qualities necessary for leadership had evaporated. After winning the Test series against India in 1967 the West Indies would not win another Test series until 1973, and would win only one Test match in that entire period, against New Zealand in 1969. A great era for West Indies cricket was over. But after a hiatus of six years, Clive Lloyd's assumption of the captaincy in the mid-1970s would mark the start of the greatest era in West Indies Test history.

SEVEN

Bajan Test Players From 1950 to 1960

Sir Everton Decourcy Weekes

Named after his father's favourite football team – 'I count my blessings that he didn't support West Bromwich Albion.' Sir Everton may be not far short of his ninetieth birthday yet he retains his mischievous sense of humour and has a permanent twinkle in his eye. Never before have I met a man with such practical optimism and such an expressive face; it can go from deeply earnest to a burst of sunshine in the blink of an eye. [He is] the only man of my acquaintance to have had a roundabout named after him. 'It's a great honour although I still have to wait in the traffic queues there.'

Julian Armfield

Frank Worrell's turn as captain was long overdue; in the same way as Everton Weekes would have been an ideal skipper for his country.

Richie Benaud

Born: Westbury, Saint Michael, Barbados, 1925
Tests: 48 (1948–1958)
Runs: 4,455
Average: 58.61
100s: 15
50s: 19
Top score: 207

At the age of ninety-one, Sir Everton DeCourcy Weekes, Knight Commander of the Order of St Michael and St George (KCMG) and holder of Barbados's Gold Crown of Merit (GCM), is the oldest surviving West Indies Test player. His batting average of 58.61 is the second highest by a West Indian and the seventh highest in the history of Test cricket.

Everton Weekes' importance to the West Indies side is reflected in the fact that he scored almost 400 runs more than Sobers in the same number of Tests. Former West Indies captain Jeff Stollmeyer gives a wonderful account of watching Everton Weekes bat:

> The other opening batsman has been dismissed and No. 4 on our scoreboard is ED Weekes. Here he comes now, a five foot six inch bundle of muscle, neatly attired, and looking good for at least 200. A wry smile to his partner and best friend (Worrell), possibly a brief greeting to the wicketkeeper, his guard is taken and right away he gets down to the business of the day. There was no nonsense about Weekes, no tomfoolery. Once on the job, he was purposeful. His business was to score runs and, believe me, Weekes liked nothing better. I hope that you have had the pleasure of seeing him score 100; this joy was mine on numerous occasions and I never tired of repetition. Each fresh boundary called forth renewed exclamations of approval. Weekes, the batsman, was an entertainer. He was businesslike, yes, but he would take a chance. He was primarily a stroke-player. Playing strokes was the game he knew and loved best, and unless circumstances warranted discretion, Weekes would produce his smashing square cut, slashing cover drive, resounding hook and forceful on-drive for all to see and enjoy.

Everton Weekes was born a quarter-mile from Bridgetown's Kensington Oval but was denied membership of its occupying club, Pickwick, as it was exclusively white at the time. His only entry to the ground was before sunrise, when he helped roll the pitch and cut the grass. "The first Test I saw was West Indies against England in 1935," recalls Weekes. "I was ten years old and stayed on after helping the ground staff, otherwise I couldn't have paid the entrance fee. I specially remember George Headley and Wally Hammond."

When he was young, Everton's cricket was confined to matches in open spaces in the neighbourhood and in the road. He first played organised cricket at the age of thirteen for Wiltshire, a team in the village league. The youngest and smallest of the players, Everton received no quarter from his seniors. "The pitches were never well prepared so you had to be innovative," he said. "The first time I got on to a properly prepared pitch I wondered just how do you get out?"

Sir Hilary Beckles quotes Weekes as saying:

> Not bad for a Westbury boy to take the number-one spot in the world [...] Maybe I was born to be a cricketer as I grew up on a street a ball's throw from the historical Kensington Oval, which loomed large in my mind as a child. It was the only place within the community that captured my imagination. There was no museum, no library; just Kensington Oval, a place of legend. I was determined to find my way out in that middle, one way or another. All of the boys in the community had the same ambition.

Sir Garfield Sobers stated that he idolized Everton Weekes because he played the game the way Sobers had always expected it to be played. Weekes was attacking, correct and never seemed to be tied down by any bowler. Frank Worrell considered Weekes to be the greatest team man, a retiring individual and a great student of the game who was never prone to finding excuses when he failed. Instead, he would look for the fault and rectify it, improving his technique as the years passed. Weekes always accepted the advice of his fellow players and was considered by Worrell to be one of the most knowledgeable individuals on the subject of cricket in the West Indies in the 1960s.

Everton Weekes debuted for the Barbados team at the age of twenty, against Trinidad and Tobago and three years later was in the West Indies' Test team. He was selected for the first three Tests against England in 1948, the first Tests played in the Caribbean after the Second World War, but was dropped after modest returns. Weekes received a last-minute call-up to replace the injured George Headley in the 4th Test in Jamaica, but an unscheduled flight stop in Puerto Rico to repair the plane's engine meant Weekes didn't arrive at Sabina Park until after lunch, when the West Indies were already in the field. Tony Cozier quotes Weekes as saying, "When I came on, I was booed all the way. The substitute who came off was JK Holt, a Jamaican favourite." But fortunes soon turned when Weekes went on to score 141. "Next day," Weekes recalls, "the same crowd came on to the field to lift me off after I got my hundred."

That century was the start of a phenomenal run of success for Weekes, being the first of five consecutive Test hundreds. He scored 141 v England in Kingston; 128 v India in Delhi; 194 v India in Bombay and 162 and 101 v India in Calcutta. Sir Everton rates his first innings 162 in Calcutta as his best: "Everywhere I tried to hit the ball, I hit it [...] To do that for four hours or thereabouts was what made it so special." In his next Test innings, in the 4th Test v India at Madras, Weekes scored 90. Ten more runs would have extended his record of five successive Test hundreds, which has never been surpassed. Weekes' innings was cut short by a run-out decision that he and Clyde Walcott described as 'rather doubtful'.

The West Indies' greatest breakthrough came when they toured England in 1950 and won the Test series 3–1. "I get fairly emotional when I talk about that tour as I felt we did so well with so little," Weekes recalled. "In fact, we'd been written off by most of the press as a pick-up side from the Caribbean." Weekes rated the batting as 'pretty strong' but noted there were no great fast bowlers, while Sonny Ramadhin and Alf Valentine were untried twenty-year-old spinners on their first tour. From then until Weekes' final Test series in 1958 they all played together for the West Indies, Weekes batting alongside Worrell and Walcott and fielding at slip or in the covers to Sonny Ramadhin and Alf Valentine.

Only Bradman performed with more consistent brilliance throughout an England tour than Weekes did in 1950, when he scored 2,310 first-class runs at an average of 79.6, including a triple-century, four double-centuries and two single-centuries. Weekes' 304 not out against Cambridge University was the highest individual first-class score by a West Indies batsman. It remains the only triple-century by a West Indian batsman on an England tour.

Former English opening batsman George Gunn, after watching Weekes score 279 runs in 235 minutes against Nottinghamshire, said, "I have seen them all since Victor Trumper and including Bradman; I have never seen a more brilliant array of strokes nor heard the ball so sweetly struck." By the end of the series Weekes had scored 1,410 Test runs at an average of 74.2 and had enhanced his reputation as one of the finest slip fielders in world cricket by taking eleven catches in the series. He was named as a *Wisden* Cricketer of the Year in 1951.

Many fans and commentators of the time consider that Weekes' most brilliant batting display was his fighting 90 in the second innings at Lord's in 1957 on a pitch so bad that the secretary of the MCC wrote him a note of congratulation and apology after the match.

Michael Manley reckoned Weekes, at his best, to be the most electrifying batsman of our age, apart from only Bradman before him and Vivian Richards after. Sir Alec Bedser (who was rated so highly by Sir Donald Bradman that he was selected in Bradman's *Greatest Test XI*) agreed, stating that once Weekes was on top there was a Bradmanian streak in his relentless pursuit of runs, his dazzling array of shots, and his pure invention.

> To hook like Weekes was seen as a sign of manliness; a sign that a batsman had become an African lion.
>
> *Grantley E Edwards*

Edwards describes Weekes as a polite and humane gentleman who is always giving pearls of wisdom. The cricketing public gravitated towards this working-class hero, who gained many disciples keen to preach the cricketing gospel according to Everton Weekes. Weekes' experience and method became the choice approach for all Bajans, such that 'poking' became a term of abuse, while playing shots all around the wicket like Weekes was met with approval.

Richie Benaud wrote that Weekes, 'set out to hammer bowlers [...] a fierce hooker, puller and square-cutter, but at the same time, a terrific driver'. Interestingly, for such a ferociously attacking player, Weekes hit only one six in his Test career of 81 innings. Weekes put this down to his upbringing: "If you hit the ball in the air and broke someone's window, you weren't getting that ball back, so we had to keep it on the ground." And he still remembers that six. The 2nd Test against Australia at Queen's Park Oval in 1955 was petering out to a draw when Weekes drove Bill Johnston over long-on. "If you only hit one six in your Test career you should remember it, shouldn't you?" he joked.

> Everton Weekes was my cricketing idol. He and I talked a lot about the game and about people. He was very laid back. He would advise and suggest but in the end he would leave it to me to do what I thought was right. He believed that if you enjoyed doing something and could benefit from it, if it was worthwhile and didn't hurt other people, then it was okay.
>
> *Sir Garfield Sobers*

Everton Weekes was thirty-two years old when he retired from Test cricket in 1958, after a series of only partially successful operations on his injured thigh muscle. For eight years after his retirement he shared with Clyde Walcott the West Indian record of 15 Test centuries, until Garry Sobers scored his 16th in 1966. Weekes led Barbados for another six years, continuing in first-class cricket until 1964, and passed 12,000 first-class runs in his final innings. He became only the third West Indian, after fellow Bajans Frank Worrell and Roy Marshall, to do so. At the age of forty, Weekes was cajoled into leading a Barbados colts team in a two-day match against the touring Australians. His class was still evident, scoring 105 before retiring at tea. After his retirement, Weekes fulfilled the roles of West Indies board member, coach, selector, team manager and ICC match referee. He also served on several government statutory boards.

Frank Worrell thought Barbados fortunate to have the services of Everton Weekes as a coach, as he was recognized throughout the cricketing world as one of the most knowledgeable men on the game: "The finer points of the game are many and varied, so it is in this aspect of the modern scientific game that a man like Everton Weekes – who has been through the mill – has his contribution to make."

Everton Weekes' average of 58.6 is second only to George Headley's 60.8 in the West Indies Test batting averages, and is seventh on the list of Test batting averages from all countries. Not far behind are fellow Bajans Frank Worrell, Weekes' friend from their pre-teen matches at the Empire Club, and Clyde Walcott.

Keith Sandiford believes that Weekes' influence on the Bajan batsmen who succeeded him was evident in the stance and mannerisms of Conrad Hunte and Seymour Nurse, both of whom showed flashes of Weekes' genius early in their careers. The torch carried by Bajan Test batsmen Carew, Hunte, Marshall and Nurse was eventually passed on to Gordon Greenidge and Desmond Haynes, in that they were gifted batsmen who could open the innings without allowing the responsibility to inhibit their strokeplay. Sandiford believes their styles emulate Weekes, even though it is unlikely that they saw him in action, Greenidge in particular appearing to have combined the techniques of Weekes with the savagery of Walcott.

Clayton Goodwin paid this tribute to Everton Weekes:

> Weekes was comparatively short in stature, with great power in his arms. He murdered any bowling but the very best, and often that as well. Weekes was particularly severe in front of the wicket and on the offside. Perhaps more than any other he had the finishing quality which is called the 'killer instinct' in boxing parlance. Once Everton decided to knock any bowler out of the attack his victim rarely survived the ordeal [...] Like Rocky Marciano – to whom his professional approach has been compared – Everton is quiet and

good-natured to everybody but his professional opponents on the field. I suspect that most West Indian fans have greater affection for him than for any other batsman of his age.

Everton Weekes was knighted for his services to cricket in 1995. In 2000 he was invited by *Wisden* to be one of the panellists to select the five greatest cricketers of the twentieth century, and he was inducted into the ICC Cricket Hall of Fame in 2009. At the time of writing Sir Everton is ninety-one years of age and living in Barbados. He still watches cricket at Kensington Oval and the Empire Club, where he blossomed into one of the greatest Test batsmen from any country, across any era.

Sir Clyde Leopold Walcott

Clyde Walcott, 'Jersey Joe' to his teammates, is built like a heavyweight champ, and hits the ball like one. Watch him crouch over the bat, knees bent, then see that colossal figure unbend and explode as he pummels the ball through the covers. His colleagues know him as one of the fiercest hitters of the ball in the game…A crisp driver on the forearm his height gave him an unbeatable advantage over everyone. Despite his size he was surprisingly nimble on his feet, and the agility he displayed behind the stumps was proof of his all-round skill as an athlete.

Ernest Eytle

Clyde Walcott would have been a great cricketer in any era…he had a unique style, a double backlift that encouraged some bowlers early in his career to believe that they had a chance of bowling him before his bat came down. They were to be disappointed.

Everton Weekes

Born: Saint Michael, Barbados, 1926
Died: Barbados, 2006
Tests: 44 (1948–1960)

Runs: 3,798
Average: 56.68
100s: 15
50s: 14
Top score: 220
Catches/stumpings: 53/11

Clyde Walcott's Test batting average is the fourth highest career average of all West Indies batsmen, behind only Headley, Weekes and Sobers. He played first-class cricket for Barbados at the age of sixteen and at the age of twenty scored 314 not out for Barbados against Trinidad, the highest individual first-class score by a Bajan batsman.

Clyde Walcott was considered to be one of the most powerful batsmen to have played Test cricket. He was able to drive with more strength off the back foot than many batsmen were able to do off the front foot and Richie Benaud reputedly wore protective gear when fielding in the gully to Walcott's batting. In the second innings of the 2nd Test at Lord's in 1950, Walcott showed he could stand comparison with Worrell and Weekes by scoring 168 not out, helping the West Indies team to its first Test victory and ultimately its first series win in England.

Walcott believed that cricket comes naturally to the West Indians and he was no exception. He was talented at other sports, representing Barbados in soccer and also playing tennis and competing in athletic events such as long jump, high jump and hurdles. When Walcott was a boy his family lived in what had once been the manager's house of a sugar estate. There, Walcott and his friends would play back-yard cricket on dirt pitches, using a breadfruit or a round stone wrapped in cloth and bound with twine as a ball. They would play for five or six hours a day, until sunset. They had no formal coaching and learned from watching others such as former Test player Derek Sealy, one of their teachers. More importantly men would join in playing, some of them leading cricketers from club sides, so the standard was high.

Walcott's father paid the fees for Clyde to join his older brother at Combermere School where he played cricket with a youngster called Frank Worrell. At the age of fourteen, Walcott moved to Harrison College, a first-grade school of which Sir Pelham Warner was a distinguished old boy. Walcott describes getting into a rut around that time, during which he could not score runs. Around that time the first team wanted a wicketkeeper and, despite having no keeping experience, he decided that the answer would be to make the first team as a wicketkeeper. He practised for one week in the nets and was asked by the sports master to keep wicket for the first team the following Saturday. In the 1941 school season Walcott hit 500 runs in 10 innings, including three centuries, and at the end of the year was invited to attend trial matches for selection of the Barbados team to visit Trinidad the following year.

Soon after his twentieth birthday, Walcott and Frank Worrell shared a world-record unbeaten 4th wicket partnership of 574 for Barbados against Trinidad. Walcott scored 314 not out and Worrell 255 not out in a stand that lasted for just under five and thee-quarter hours. Walcott later recalled that the Trinidadian crowd 'fell over themselves' with excitement at their batting, the endearing quality of a West Indies crowd being that, provided there was plenty of action, they did not much care about the result.

Simon Lister relates a wonderful story of Bajan poet Kamau Brathwaite describing a Walcott innings against England at Kensington Oval, shortly after the Second World War. Walcott had just hit a four. "'You see dat shot?' the people was shoutin'; 'Jesus Chrise, man, wunna see dat shot?' All over de groun' fellers shakin' hands wid each other as if was they wheelin' de willow as if was them had the power; one man run out pun de field wid a red fowl cock goin' quawk quawk quawk in 'e han'; woulda give it to Clyde right then an' right there if a police hadn't stop 'e!" Lister summarised that Clyde Walcott was scoring his runs for a nation; those runs belonged to the people and they knew it.

Walcott recalls that even after he had started playing at a first-class level, cricket gear was scarce and expensive. He couldn't afford more than one pair of battings gloves and was playing Test cricket before he owned his first pair of pads. The bat with which he scored his highest first-class score (314 not out in 1946) had two straps across it, glued to the bat to prevent cracks. There was a shortage of rubber after the war, so his bat handle was encased in chamois leather held in place at the top and bottom with twine.

Clyde Walcott was an underrated wicketkeeper when he began his Test career, but he learned quickly. He considered English wicketkeeper Godfrey Evans to be the greatest keeper of his era and, being conscious of how much he had to learn, watched Evans closely when the English side toured in 1948. Walcott discussed equipment and technique with Evans and felt he was a much better wicketkeeper when the MCC returned home in 1948 than when they arrived.

Walcott speculated in his book *Island Cricketers* that former West Indies captain Jeff Stollmeyer was probably not one of his fans. However, that is not evident in Stollmeyer's book *Everything Under the Sun*, wherein Stollmeyer had nothing but praise for Walcott. Stollmeyer wrote that Walcott improved immeasurably as a wicketkeeper over the years and in time graduated to the front rank of Test keepers. Strong and safe, his reach enabled him to make catches that other keepers would not consider attempting.

Stollmeyer believed that Walcott was of immense value to the West Indies team on two tours; India in 1948/49 and England in 1950. Apart from his responsibilities as wicketkeeper, Walcott was the West Indies' number-three batsman in India. He carried the batting of the team on his shoulders during the early stages of the tour, playing more than one crisis Test innings. In England he scored seven centuries, most of them at a time when runs were most urgently needed. In the first Test match at Old Trafford, in the absence through injury of HH Johnson, Walcott took time off from keeping wicket to open the bowling.

One of Walcott's chief strengths was his ability to hit the ball with explosive power off both the front and back foot. Stollmeyer wrote that Walcott's driving, straight and through the covers, during his innings of 168 not out in the Lord's Test of 1950 will long be remembered by those who were fortunate enough to witness it. Walcott could hook off the front foot and was one of the few batsmen who could take fast bowling by the scruff of its neck and tear it apart. He was the best hooker of pace bowling that Frank Worrell had seen and the only one Worrell had witnessed hooking forward of square-leg.

In 1951 Walcott and Worrell shared the highest 5th wicket partnership (189) against New Zealand. In the 1953/54 series against England, Walcott scored 698 Test runs at an average of 87.25, including three centuries, one of which was a double-century. In the 2nd Test in Barbados the West Indies were against the wall; Weekes was out of the side through injury and Walcott came in with the innings in tatters. Walcott changed the course of the game by scoring 220 out of a total of 383.

By the mid-1950s, Clyde Walcott was one of the world's leading batsmen. He had a remarkable series in 1954/55 against Australia, where he set two world records. The first was twice scoring a century in each innings of a Test in the same series: at Port of Spain, Trinidad (126 and 110) and Kingston, Jamaica (155 and 110). And the second was scoring five centuries in the same Test series. Walcott scored 827 runs from ten Test innings, while most of his teammates failed against the pace of Lindwall and Miller.

In 1957/58 Walcott shared a record 4th wicket partnership of 188 with fellow Bajan Garry Sobers against Pakistan, in Jamaica, and was selected as a *Wisden* Cricketer of the Year in 1958. Walcott retired from Test cricket in 1960 and from first-class cricket in 1964.

Clyde Walcott had a keen sense of humour. Eytle relates a story that during the match between the West Indies and South Australia on the 1950/51 tour, Frank Worrell had been clean bowled first ball. Before going out to bat in the second innings Worrell had superstitiously shed every garment of clothing he had worn in the first innings and clad himself in brand new gear. Worrell faced his first ball and was bowled, for a 'pair'. As the incoming batsman

Walcott passed Worrell on the pavilion steps he laughed, "Why do I have to face a hat-trick every time I follow you?"

In 1963, Everton Weekes, who until 1966 shared with Walcott the West Indian record of 15 Test centuries, reflected:

> It was always a great pleasure to bat with either Frank [Worrell] or Clyde [Walcott]; although Clyde openly stated in Australia in 1951 that he was only ranked with the other Ws because his name started with W also. Of course I know better than that because I have Clyde very high up on my batting list and I dare say that many of the great bowlers of our time will readily agree that Clyde was a batsman of the highest order. The game has not produced many players who hit the ball harder off the back foot and on the up. Clyde, I am certain, will admit that he was not a technician, but he certainly had as much punch as Sonny Liston.

After his retirement, Clyde Walcott was a leading figure in moulding Guyana into a cricketing force and assisting the development of Guyanese players such as Basil Butcher, Lance Gibbs, Alvin Kallicharran, Rohan Kanhai and Clive Lloyd. In 1966 Walcott was awarded an OBE for services to cricket in Barbados, Guyana and the West Indies. He was chairman of the West Indies selectors from 1973 to 1988 and managed the West Indies teams that won World Cups in 1975, 1979 and 1987. Walcott was president of the West Indies Cricket Board from 1988 to 1993, was appointed an International Cricket Council match referee in 1992 and became chairman of the International Cricket Council in 1997, the first black man to hold the position.

In 1983 Walcott was selected by the Lord's Taverners as one of the fifty greatest Test cricketers since the Second World War. He was awarded the Barbados Gold Crown of Merit in 1991, became a Knight of St Andrew in the Order of Barbados in 1993, and in 1994 was knighted for services to cricket. Sir Clyde Walcott died on 26 August 2006, in Bridgetown, Barbados.

Sir Frank Mortimer Maglinne Worrell

> Worrell's unobtrusive skill, his reserve and his dignity on the field made him a great favourite with the British public who saw in him the embodiment of qualities which they admired. And with the Australian public it was the same.
>
> *CLR James*

> When in the New Year's Honours of 1964 the Queen bestowed a knighthood on the cricketer known all over the world as Frankie Worrell, an honour was done to cricket and to a great gentleman, who did not acquire the knightly qualities – courage, courtesy and the gift of leading – for the first time on that January morning. These gifts had been bestowed upon him at birth forty years before and were already developing in the eager boy who first played cricket in his native island of Barbados...wherever he now goes, and whatever he does, English cricket salutes a great gentleman.
>
> *AA Thomson*

Born: Saint Michael, Barbados, 1924
Died: Kingston, Jamaica, 1967
Tests: 51 (1948–1963)
Runs: 3,860
Average: 49.48
100s: 9
50s: 22
Top score: 261
Wickets: 69
Bowling average: 38.72
5 wickets in innings: 2

Jeff Stollmeyer gave the following account of watching a Frank Worrell innings:

> One of the openers is out and there is a hush of expectancy among the spectators. A lithe athletic figure emerges from the pavilion

and a prolonged cheer greets his arrival on to the playing area. He walks with head down, rather quickly and somewhat apologetically to the crease, the bat held in his left hand. As he passes the not-out batsman, he smiles, rubs his eyes (he has been sleeping in the dressing room for the last hour) and stammers laughingly, "Wha-wha-what's going on out here, old man?" In due course, he takes his guard, has a word or two with the wicketkeeper and nearest fieldsman and then prepares himself for the fun of the day. Frank Worrell has started another innings. If it has been your good fortune to see a hundred from Worrell you will have seen batsmanship of the highest class. Classic late cuts, drives off the back foot through mid-on, hooks and straight drives all enchantingly played and executed with precision and wrists of steel.

Frank Worrell was the first black cricketer to captain the West Indies for an entire Test series. When he was a child in Barbados his family home overlooked the famous Empire Cricket Ground, and from an early age Worrell took an interest in what was happening across the way. He attended Combermere secondary school, where his bowling efforts were spotted by one of the masters, former Test player Derek Sealy. Sealy had played his first Test match at the age of seventeen and was adept at recognizing promise in young players. He took the bold step of putting the thirteen-year-old Worrell into the First XI, to the annoyance of the older boys and some of the masters.

During his time at Combermere Worrell developed the habit of taking a nap during his team's innings. He would put on his pads, find a quiet corner and sink into a deep sleep until it was his turn to bat. He never shook the habit, as it helped to dissipate the nervous moments before going in to bat. During a Test match Worrell never read a newspaper or magazine; he merely slept. Wes Hall confirmed that Worrell slept through Rohan Kanhai's momentous innings in the final Test against England in 1963, and on several occasions had to be hurriedly woken up with the incoming batsman already mounting the pavilion steps. While that habit may have raised eyebrows all those years ago, Worrell was actually ahead of his time. What he was doing then was merely his version of the relaxation techniques taught today by sports psychologists, through meditation and self-hypnosis.

Worrell once told CLR James that, as a young man, he could tell exactly where a ball was going to drop as soon as it had left the bowler's hand. This talent shone early. When he was nineteen, Worrell scored 308 not out against Trinidad in a world-record partnership of 502 in just under six and three-quarter hours with fellow Bajan and future West Indies captain John Goddard. Clyde Walcott recounted that for all the runs and records from that stand, one amusing incident stood out in his mind. Jeff Stollmeyer, opening the Trinidad innings, had hit his own highest score of 210, and when Worrell passed that mark one of the spectators ran onto the pitch and presented him with a large white chicken.

Two years later, again against Trinidad, Worrell scored 255 not out in a world-record unbeaten 4th wicket stand of 574 with Clyde Walcott. Walcott later recalled that he and Worrell 'thoroughly enjoyed' themselves and that Worrell, the idol of the Trinidad crowd, spent a large part of the five and three-quarter hours whistling and singing happily to himself.

Not everything about life in Barbados was rosy for Worrell, who admitted in later years that he was not particularly amenable to any form of discipline and that his high-school years were psychologically hard. By the time he reached fourth form he was under such strain that he had developed a persecution complex. At the age of twenty-three Worrell left Barbados to live in Jamaica and the following year he went to England to play for Radcliffe in the Central Lancashire League. Worrell played for Radcliffe for the next twelve years and was also employed as coach to the club and other outside teams. Worrell believed that it was possible to learn more in three years of league cricket than it was in twelve years of cricket outside the UK, even at an international level, in that one had to learn to cope with the swerving ball, turning ball and cutter.

CLR James theorized that the twentieth century saw three captains who expressed a certain stage of cricket and a certain stage of society and that without some grasp of what each of those players represented 'cricket is just a lot of men hitting a ball and running about in flannels'. Those captains were Pelham (Plum) Warner, Donald Bradman and Frank Worrell. Plum Warner, from 1903 until the start of the Second World War, took the game of cricket all over the world. Bradman, from 1928 until just after the end of the Second World War, incorporated every technique the game had invented and adapted it to defeating an opponent. And the man who broke this pattern, and made it clear that the game should return to what it had once been, was Frank Worrell.

Richie Benaud was of a similar view, but substituted CB Fry for Plum Warner, stating that Fry dominated the first twenty years of the twentieth century, similarly Bradman before 1948 and Frank Worrell after 1960. Author RS Whitington said, "Asked in 1953 which of the world's batsmen past or present he would choose to give an exhibition of stroke-play at the London Palladium, our old friend Charles Burgess Fry said, 'Frank Worrell without a doubt.'" Given that this is the one and the same CB Fry whom Richie Benaud considered to be the dominant cricketing figure of the first twenty years of the twentieth century, that was a huge endorsement for Worrell.

Sir Alec Bedser described Worrell as the quintessence of elegance; superior on wet or turning pitches, fluent in stroke and movement with a grace in his unhurried, easy power. He never hit across the line of the ball or panicked. His quick brain and judgment were his main allies and he was a born leader, unifying the scattered West Indies islands and setting exemplary standards in every sense.

Worrell was also possessed of a strong sense of justice. When he asked for a modest amount of money to tour India, the West Indies cricket board refused to negotiate. Showing his leadership skills, Worrell refused to back down, serving notice that black professionals would no longer be prepared to be exploited. Cricket was their life and they were entitled for it to be their livelihood. Michael Manley believed that this act was significant in two ways. First, it marked Worrell as a man of principle. Secondly, it set him apart and made him special in the eyes of his compatriots and colleagues, in that he had that something extra that 'makes men pioneers'.

Eytle sums up the manner in which Worrell garnered his players' respect:

> Neat, affable, always dapper and seldom seen without a disarming smile [...] Frank is reserved, yet friendly, enjoying life to the full. He is tremendous fun at a party and is always happy until the talk turns to cricket, then he slides away to a corner, preferring to talk of other things [...] Like most of his teammates his sense of discipline is strong, but he never restricted the movements of his players. He left it to their own good sense to retire at a reasonable time and allow themselves sufficient rest for the job in hand. By his own example he got results, and no one would be foolish enough to let such a skipper down.

Wes Hall confirmed Eytle's sentiments, stating that the quiet dignity of Worrell had done more than anything to uphold the reputation of West Indies cricket in foreign lands. While socially Worrell was a charming, friendly fellow who sincerely meant every word he said, on the field he was 'a cold-blooded tracker – a killer with dignity'. He expected his dignity to spread through his team and had a unique theory on wicket-taking: 'Above all remain calm [...] running about shaking hands and kissing each other like footballers only creates an impression that we are not used to taking wickets.'

Frank Worrell was the first black cricketer to captain the West Indies Test team for an entire series, leading them on notable tours to Australia in 1960/61 and England in 1963. Manley summarized the moment when Worrell was chosen, at the age of thirty-six, to undertake the onerous task of leading the tour to Australia:

> Frank Mortimer Maglinne Worrell...was to undertake the challenge that goes with this honour not in the comparative security of his own backyard, but from the cricketing point of view, in the most hostile terrain in the world, a tour of Australia. He was to lead the third West Indian side into this forbidden territory in the knowledge that the two earlier expeditions had ended in resounding defeats.

Tony Cozier believed that Worrell's seniority may actually have been an advantage, in that the disparity in age between Worrell and his teammates generated an affection and respect which a younger captain may have found impossible to maintain. Worrell had established a considerable reputation as a player and, despite his age, had proved his worth with both bat and ball. As such, he was able to transform the West Indies team from a loose band of cricketers into a professional outfit.

Alan McGilvray gave some insight into an incident which may have motivated Worrell on the 1960/61 Australian tour. McGilvray considered that Everton Weekes, a close friend of Worrell's, had been unfairly targeted by Australian fast bowlers Lindwall and Miller in the last Test of the 1950/51 Test series, and he publicly said so. McGilvray suspected that Frank Worrell probably felt the same and that by the time he returned to Australia for the 1960/61 tour he was totally committed to winning and competing with Australia on its own terms.

Worrell was a great tactician, as Hall recollected when writing about Worrell's captaincy during the 3rd Test against Australia in 1961. Australian batsmen Norm O'Neill and Neil Harvey seemed set to lead Australia to victory, but Harvey was suffering from a pulled muscle in his right leg. Worrell reckoned this could be a handicap against a spinner, so he brought Sobers close in at cover and told finger-spinner Lance Gibbs to flight the ball at Harvey. Gibbs did as instructed and Harvey went out to drive. But with his injured leg he could not get to the pitch of the ball and was caught in the covers. Gibbs took 5 for 66 and the West Indies won the Test by 222 runs.

In September 1961 Worrell, who by now had his university degree, took up duties as warden of Irvine, a hall of residence at the University College of West Indies. His role was to provide leadership and guidance to the students and assist in the planning of sports and recreation.

Worrell shouldered the job of leading the West Indies to England in 1963 and achieved success as spectacular as that achieved in Australia two years earlier. Upon the conclusion of the 1963 English tour Worrell was appointed to the Jamaican Senate, which had been established upon Jamaica attaining independence in 1963. The Senate was modelled on the English House of Lords, in that its unpaid membership incorporated a cross-section of the community. Worrell is the only Bajan-born citizen to have been so honoured.

Frank Worrell was knighted in 1964, becoming only the fourth Test cricketer at that time (behind Englishmen Hobbs and Hutton and Australian Bradman) to have been knighted. In the same year he left Jamaica for Trinidad, where he took up an offer from the Prime Minister to act as a consultant on community development. Once in Trinidad he also took up a position as dean of students and warden at the St Augustine campus of the University of Trinidad.

In December 1966 Worrell undertook a six-week tour of India, at the invitation of the Indian government. But he was not well, feeling constantly tired and irritable. At the end of the tour he flew back to Jamaica, where he was familiar with the university hospital and staff, for a check-up. By the time Worrell arrived in Jamaica he was too ill even for a haircut and had to be taken to the hospital ward in a wheelchair. There he was diagnosed with leukaemia and given as little as six weeks to live. Worrell told a journalist at *The Gleaner* that only his courage had carried him through India. Sir Frank Worrell died on 13 March 1967, only a few weeks after he had appeared to be in good health.

When the news of Frank Worrell's death reached Barbados the flags were lowered to half-mast. So much condolence mail arrived at Mona that a secretary had to be assigned to deal with it. One of Worrell's biographers, Ivo Tennant, wrote that a telegram from Queen Elizabeth II read, 'I am extremely sorry to hear of the sad death of Frank Worrell. Please convey my sympathies to his widow.' Sir Frank Worrell is buried at the University of the West Indies in Barbados with his wife Velda and his daughter Lana who, at the time of her death, was married to Clyde Walcott's son Michael.

Tennant believed that generosity was one of Worrell's finest traits. He gave items of his cricket kit to students and poor children in Boys' Town, Kingston and donated money to universities, individuals and causes. He supplied two teams in the Jamaican Netball Association with gear and uniforms and paid their affiliation and league fees. CLR James described Worrell as a combination of the most unusual gifts, being possessed of an almost unbridled passion for social equality and always most concerned with the welfare of the men in his side who had no social status. His men repaid him with fanatical devotion and he was to the West Indian population an authentic national hero. Ironically, it was Worrell who had proclaimed in the early 1960s that Barbados had no national hero.

Many sportsmen give weight to the way in which they are judged by their peers; those who understand the pressures involved in top-level sport and the mental strength needed to succeed. By all accounts, Frank Worrell's peers considered him one of the greatest men to have graced the game, describing him as brave, humble, honest and dignified. His tremendous influence on West Indies cricket was such that he became the role model for later captains such as Sobers, Kanhai, Lloyd and Richards. The esteem in which Sir Frank Worrell was and is still held is reflected in the following tributes.

> Frank [Worrell] and Clyde [Walcott] apart from being great cricketers, were great gentlemen who never hesitated to give the youngsters the benefit of their experience. Frank in particular is of a very generous nature and has helped players both off and on the field with problems.
>
> *Everton Weekes*
>
> Worrell is one of the few who after a few hours of talk have left me as tired as if I had been put through a wringer. His responses to difficult questions were so unhesitating, so precise, and so took the subject on to unsuspected but relevant areas, that I felt it was I who was undergoing examination. No cricketer, and I have talked to many, ever shook me up in a similar manner.
>
> *CLR James*

[Worrell's] uncanny way of drawing a team together healed the one wound in West Indies cricket. For years the players from Barbados, Jamaica, Trinidad and British Guiana had stayed in their own private cliques, whether they were swimming on the beach or at a social function. With the Caribbean Islands so scattered I suppose it was natural, but it did not help to create any sort of team spirit. Under Frank this narrow outlook disappeared. He welded us into one big, happy family, an achievement which will be a lasting memory of a great skipper.

Wes Hall

Frank Worrell [was] in every sense of the word one of the greatest cricketers the world has known…Apart from being a great cricketer, he was a wonderful leader of men, and few in the history of cricket have had a better influence on the game and on other people…Frank Worrell remains the best person I have ever seen in man-management. Frank was the first black West Indian cricketer to be allowed to captain a team away from the Caribbean and he was one of the reasons the face of cricket in Australia, and perhaps in other parts of the world, changed forever because of that tied Test series. No one but Worrell, and I mean no one, could have done it for the West Indies. He remains one of the outstanding people I have met. I hope he continues to be revered in the West Indies as well. His passing was a great sadness for those who knew him and admired him for all he had done for West Indies cricket and the people of the West Indies.

Richie Benaud

Sir Garfield St Auburn Sobers

[Sobers] was a supreme artiste whose fan base in Bridgetown and beyond was fanatical about his stagecraft. For many, he possessed the performance magic. His movements were bold, beautiful and awe-inspiring…His kingdom stretched from the island to England; from India to Australia; from New Zealand to Pakistan;

and from South Africa to the black diaspora...He was the most world-famous Bajan of his time, a household global name captured in verse and calypso.

Sir Hilary Beckles

Garfield St Aubrun Sobers is so extraordinary a cricketer that if we hadn't known him it would have been ridiculous to invent him.

JS Barker

Born: Bridgetown, Barbados, 1936
Tests: 93 (1954–1974)
Runs: 8,032
Average: 57.78
100s/50s: 26/30
Top score: 365 n.o.
Wickets: 235
Bowling average: 34.03
5 wickets in innings: 6
Best bowling: 6/73
Catches: 109

Garfield (Garry) Sobers was only five years old when his father died on a ship which had been torpedoed by a German U-Boat. Sobers was born with an extra finger on each hand, considered by some Bajans as a good luck omen. One of the extra fingers came off when he was nine or ten, with the help of a piece of catgut wrapped around the base of the finger, and Sobers played his first colonial game with eleven fingers. He removed the other with the help of a sharp knife when he was fourteen or fifteen years old, as he was by then playing serious cricket.

Sobers is universally acknowledged as the greatest Test all-rounder in history. His Test batting average of 57.78 is the third highest of all West Indies batsmen, behind only George Headley and Everton Weekes, and the fourth highest in the list of cricketers with more than 5,000 Test runs. In addition, he took 235 Test wickets.

Richie Benaud described Sobers as 'a brilliant batsman, splendid fielder, particularly close to the wicket, and a bowler of extraordinary skill, whether bowling with the new ball, providing orthodox left-arm spin or over-the-wrist spin'. Alan McGilvray remembers Sobers as a batsman who destroyed bowlers; a ruthless carnivore who would simply gobble up the finest bowlers of his time, as if they existed only to be his fodder.

In 1958, at the age of twenty-one, Sobers scored a world-record Test score of 365 not out against Pakistan at Sabina Park, Jamaica. He batted for just over ten hours; three hours less than English opener Len Hutton had batted in setting the previous record of 364. Sobers' score remained the Test world-record for thirty-six years until West Indian Brian Lara scored 375 in 1994. His partnership of 446 with fellow Bajan Conrad Hunte was the second highest for any wicket in Test cricket and they were only the fourth pair to bat throughout a complete day of Test cricket.

In the 4th Test of the same series, Sobers scored a century in each innings (125 and 109 not out) and shared a 2nd wicket partnership of 269 with Clyde Walcott. These innings took his aggregate in three Test innings to 599, for only one dismissal. Sobers made 824 Test runs in that series, including three consecutive centuries, followed by 557 Test runs and three centuries on the West Indies tour of India in 1958/59. By the 3rd Test of the Indian series Sobers had scored six centuries in as many Tests.

In September 1959, Sobers' good friend and fellow West Indies Test batsman Collie Smith was killed when the car in which they were travelling was involved in an accident. Sobers admitted in his autobiography that he was deeply affected by his friend's death for some time. But he eventually decided that he would be letting his country down if he 'disappeared into the mists of an alcoholic haze'. So Sobers resolved to play for Collie Smith as well, setting himself the arduous task of playing Test cricket for two men.

In the 1959/60 series against England, Sobers scored 709 Test runs, including three centuries. In the 1st Test in Barbados, Sobers

(226) and Worrell (197 not out) played the two longest innings against England. Their partnership of 399 in 579 minutes remains the West Indies 4th wicket record and was at that time the longest partnership in Test cricket.

Inspired by the new West Indies captain Frank Worrell, Sobers had an outstanding 1960/61 series in Australia. He scored a scintillating 132 runs in just over 120 minutes on the first day of the tied Test. Richie Benaud recalled:

> Sobers played a wonderful innings, fuelled a little by the newspaper article on the first morning which suggested he might have a few problems with my bowling. He had none. Take my word for that! He played an innings which I put into the top bracket of anything I have seen, an explosive exhibition of stroke-play and power which, in the context of the disappointing tour to that date, was magnificent.

Sobers was selected as a *Wisden* Cricketer of the Year in 1964 and succeeded the retired Frank Worrell as West Indies' captain for the 1964/65 series against Australia. He was an immediate success as captain when, in March 1965, the West Indies defeated Australia by 179 runs in the 1st Test in Jamaica. In the same Test (his 48th) Sobers became the first player to score 4,000 runs and take 100 wickets in Test cricket. The West Indies won the series 2–1 and claimed the Frank Worrell Trophy, the first time the West Indies had beaten Australia in a Test series.

Sobers had spectacular success on the West Indies' 1966 tour of England. In the 2nd Test at Lord's, Sobers (163 not out) and his Bajan cousin David Holford (105 not out) shared an unbroken partnership of 274, which remains the highest 6th wicket partnership in Tests at Lord's. At Leeds, Sobers became the first player to score a century and take five wickets in a single innings during the same Test, on two occasions (having previously done so against India in Jamaica in 1962).

In the five Test matches of the 1966 tour, which the West Indies won 3–1, Sobers scored 722 runs at an average of 103.14, including three centuries. JS Barker wrote that after Sobers had completed the first of his three centuries, the England short-leg fielder Colin 'Ollie' Milburn reportedly said to him, "You know something, Garry? You're ruining this bloody game!"

On that tour Sobers also took 20 wickets at an average of 27.2 and thus became the first all-rounder to achieve the 'double' of 700 runs and 20 wickets in a Test series. At the conclusion of the 1967/68 series against England in the West Indies, Sobers became the first player to score 6,000 runs and take 150 wickets in Test cricket. After 65 Tests his batting average was 63.8, the second highest behind Donald Bradman.

> The most dangerous ball to a left-hander was the ball from a fast-medium or a fast bowler which hit on the off-stump or middle and off and went away. To this particular ball, Sobers developed a scoring stroke. From the back foot he put it away past cover's right hand, and such was his precision and timing and mastery that round about the stroke grew the phrase: 'Not a man moved!'
>
> CLR James

In April 1971, Sobers took his 200th Test wicket in his 80th Test. He became the first player to achieve 7,000 runs and 200 wickets in Test cricket and only the second all-rounder, after Richie Benaud, to score more than 2,000 Test runs and take more than 200 Test wickets.

In January 1972, Sobers scored 254 in the 3rd unofficial Test between Australia and the Rest of the World XI at the Melbourne Cricket Ground. Sir Donald Bradman said of the innings:

> It was an incredible innings, full of the most savage power, the most brilliant shots, the most delicate placements – some of his footwork was absolutely perfect; at other times even when his feet were not absolutely in the right place, the ball still sped off the bat to the boundary with such speed that it left the field man standing

like stumps [...] I count myself privileged to have been there and to have had the opportunity of commenting on this innings which will live in the minds of all who saw it for as long as life should last.

In March 1972, Sobers scored his 7,460th Test run to surpass Colin Cowdrey and become the leading run scorer in Test cricket. The following month Sobers played his 85th consecutive Test match, a world record. He had not missed playing in a Test match since April 1955, seventeen years earlier.

In February 1974, Sobers and Bernard Julien shared a partnership of 112 for the 6th wicket against England, in Jamaica. This was Sobers' 43rd century partnership in Tests, a new record. This innings set another world record for Sobers, when he became the first batsman to score 8,000 Test runs. Although other batsmen have since exceeded that total, Sobers remains the only cricketer to have scored 8,000 runs and taken 200 wickets in Test cricket.

Sandiford considers that Sobers was the player who learnt most from the Three Ws and then surpassed them all. He was strong off the back foot and could improvise strokes beyond the capacity of most other batsmen, his flick through midwicket off the back foot being an impossible stroke for most other batsmen.

> From a very high back-lift he watches the ball that is barely over the good length, [Sobers] takes it on the rise and sends it shooting between mid-on and mid-off...The West Indian crowd has a favourite phrase for that stroke: 'Not a man moved!'
>
> *CLR James*

Garry Sobers retired from Test cricket in 1974 and was knighted in the following year for his services to cricket. In 1998 he was named as one of only ten national heroes of Barbados. In 2000 he was selected as one of *Wisden*'s Cricketers of the twentieth century, amassing the second highest number of votes (90), behind only Sir Donald Bradman (100).

In 2007, *Wisden* retrospectively selected the leading cricketer in the world for every year dating back to 1900 (excepting the years during the world wars). Sobers was selected for eight years (1958, 1960, 1962, 1964, 1965, 1966, 1968 and 1970). Only Sobers and Bradman (10) received the accolade more than three times.

In 2010, English sports journalist Richard Sydenham published *In a League of their Own: 100 Cricket Legends Select Their World XI*. Ninety of the hundred contributors selected Sobers in their greatest side and he was selected in the final All Time World XI. Only Sir Donald Bradman received more votes.

> Is Sobers the 'greatest' of all all-round cricketers even? Performance, in any calling of life, is related to environment, to the material pressures which, to some extent, 'condition' even genius. Maybe Sobers could have coped with the terrible 'sticky' wickets which Victor Trumper conquered triumphantly in 1902, against some of the finest spinners in cricket's history. But we cannot measure genius with genius; you cannot try to place a Mozart above a Beethoven, a Bach above a Schubert. Each is an *absolute*.
>
> *Neville Cardus*

Sir Wesley Winfield Hall

> One of the most characteristic and loved of all cricketers, Hall was among the fastest of bowlers and put the fear of God into batsmen the world over for a decade from the late 1950s. Operating from an intimidatingly long run and with a gold crucifix thumping against his torso, he made a thrilling spectacle as he spearheaded the West Indies attack for his captain, muse and protector, Frank Worrell.
>
> *Mike Coward*

Fast bowlers come in all shapes, styles and temperaments. Few have been as near to the ideal image as Wesley Hall. He bowled his heart out for a decade from 1958 in which he terrorised the Indians, overwhelmed the English and startled the Australians. The picture of him trudging back, shirt tail out over his trousers, mopping the sweat from his brow, for just one more over when others would have given up long ago, whether it was in Adelaide, Kingston or Lord's, is one of cricket's most abiding memories.

Clayton Goodwin

With one of the longest run-ups in the history of the game, he bounded to the wicket – a sight of terror. Six feet three inches tall and proportionately wide, all of it sinew, he steamed in with the gallop of a long-jumper. His eyes bulged, teeth glinted, the characteristic crucifix flew ahead propelled by the hurtling pace. Finally came the leap accompanied by arms flailing about as in a cartwheel, and the ball was released at well over 90 miles per hour.

Arunabha Sengupta

Born: Saint Michael, Barbados, 1937
Tests: 48 (1958–1969)
Wickets: 192
Bowling average: 26.38
5 wickets in innings: 9
10 wickets in match: 1
Best bowling: 7/69

Wes Hall describes his early life as being tough:

> Life is a drama. I had great problems throughout my life. I was raised by a single-parent family. I did not have the luxury of a father in the home, or a man for that matter. It was the five of us – my mother, grandmother, aunt, brother and I. That was my world [...] If you are living in a chattel house with no electricity, no radio, no pipe water and a pit toilet in the yard, you have to aspire to get to high school [...] In those days, there was no free education. I had to win a scholarship [...] I got to Combermere. I knew that was the only hope for me [...] I have sprung from the proletariat. I only

had two ambitions as a boy. I wanted to go to Combermere and to play for West Indies. It is true that in 1944 that would appear to be a Herculean task.

Hall attended Combermere School at the time when the leading schools in Barbados played against adults in Division 1 of the Barbados Cricket Association, and so was exposed to a high standard of cricket at an early age. It was not long before he was selected to play for the West Indies, an event he describes as the most defining moment in his life.

In 1959, Hall took a hat-trick in a Test against Pakistan, the first West Indian cricketer to do so. The 1960/61 Test series against Australia is one of the most famous in the history of cricket and Hall played a major role in its outcome. The first Test in Brisbane was the tied Test, in which Hall bowled the final over. *Wisden* said of Hall's effort that he bowled as though he meant to take a wicket with every delivery. Hall bowled 17 eight-ball overs on the final day, including the sensational last one in which three wickets fell.

On the 1963 tour of England, Hall formed a lethal opening bowling attack with fellow Bajan Charlie Griffith. One of Hall's greatest performances was in the 2nd Test at Lord's when, on the final day, he bowled unchanged for 200 minutes, broken only by the tea interval. As in the tied Test in Brisbane three years earlier Hall, having toiled manfully all day, bowled the final over with both sides still capable of winning. Hall bowled 40 overs in the innings and took 4/93, claiming it as his 'finest hour'.

The tussle at Lord's between English captain Ted Dexter and Hall and Griffith were among the most thrilling in post-war cricket. Dexter's innings of 70, in not much more than even time, was considered by many who witnessed it to be one of the finest innings they had seen against such hostile bowling and possibly the best Test innings not to have been rewarded with a century. On the final day Colin Cowdrey's arm was broken by a ball from Hall which 'kicked'. Then, in poor light, Brian Close took a fearful barrage of blows to his body and led England to within sight of a possible victory. A famous photograph taken after the game shows a shirtless Close covered in black and blue, cricket-ball sized bruises, colloquially known to Bajans as 'blue duppies'.

Goodwin summed up the performances of Hall and Griffith on the 1963 tour:

> Batsmen are usually more likely to hit the headlines than bowlers, but in 1963 Hall and Griffith were the centre of attraction and the key to victory. England had not been tested so severely before by West Indian fast bowlers, and were not so again until they came up against Andy Roberts, Michael Holding and Wayne Daniel in 1976 [...] The picture of Wesley Hall in full flow as he ran towards the wicket is still treasured in the memories of all but the opposing batsmen – and maybe in theirs as well – and the thought of Griffith's bouncers mixed with the yorker can yet disturb his former opponents' sleep.

Wes Hall was one of the most popular cricketers of his era, particularly in Australia. Australian commentator Johnnie Moyes described Hall as, 'a rare box-office attraction, a man who caught and held the affections of the paying public.' But even though Hall loved Australia and had many friends there, he was not afraid to voice his honest opinion about certain aspects of the social conditions that existed in Australia in the 1960s, once candidly telling Australian Prime Minister Sir Robert Menzies that he was 'not too amused' by the White Australia Policy.

Wear and tear on his body saw Hall retire in 1969, his final wickets tally being an impressive192 wickets at an average of 26.4. After retiring from cricket, Hall entered Bajan politics, serving in the Barbados Senate and the House of Assembly and being appointed Minister of Tourism in 1987. "If you think my run-up was long, you should hear my speeches," he once quipped. He was also involved in the administration of West Indies cricket as a selector and team manager.

In 1990 Hall made what he called 'a very serious decision to give heart and life to God' when he attended Bible school and was later ordained a minister in the Christian Pentecostal Church. Hall stated, "My mother was a leading light in that respect [...] She mentored me. I had a Christian upbringing. I gave my life to the Lord twenty-four years ago. Some people said I couldn't last three weeks, some said three months. I'm so pleased that God has been good to me continuously. I feel that was the best decision I ever made in my life." In a sad final reunion of two of the finest ever Bajan and West Indies fast bowlers, Hall ministered Malcolm Marshall in the final days of his terminal illness.

In 2001 Hall was elected president of the West Indies Cricket Board and was instrumental in ensuring that the 2007 Cricket World Cup was held in the West Indies. Hall is a member of the ICC Cricket Hall of Fame and the West Indies Cricket Hall of Fame.

Wesley Hall was knighted in 2012, becoming only the second specialist bowler, after Sir Alec Bedser, to be so honoured (Lord Learie Constantine's 1962 knighthood was conferred primarily due to his work as a lawyer, politician and diplomat). Hall was perceived by his opponents as a good-hearted person, Ted Dexter recounting, "There was never a hint of malice in him or in his bowling." Frank Worrell once said of Hall, "Unlike most fast bowlers, (Hall) discusses cricket in all other terms except the first person singular. There is not the least trace of egotism in the man." When Australian wicketkeeper Wally Grout's jaw was broken by a delivery from Hall, no one was more distressed than Hall himself.

Hall's camaraderie and zest for life endeared him to fans in the West Indies, Australia and England alike. He once scored a first-class century against Cambridge University and in his typically humorous fashion recalled, "But it wasn't any old hundred – it was against the intelligentsia!"

Sir Conrad Cleophas Hunte

> No one, except Sir Frank Worrell, has done as much as Conrad Hunte to convey to a wider world the impression of the modern West Indian as a first-class citizen and sportsman.
>
> *EW Swanton*

Conrad Hunte reinforced an early impression – a very sophisticated, assured man of the world, but still young enough to smile spontaneously and naturally.

CLR James

Born: Saint Andrew, Barbados, 1932
Died: Sydney, Australia, 3 December 1999
Tests: 44 (1958–1967)
Runs: 3,245
Average: 45.06
100s/50s: 8/13
Top score: 260

Conrad Hunte was the most reliable opening batsman produced by the West Indies until the appearances of Gordon Greenidge and Desmond Haynes in the 1970s. He was the eldest of nine children and as a child lived in a one-room wooden shack on the sugar plantation where his father worked. Determined that his son would receive a good education, Hunte senior made Conrad walk three miles every day, in bare feet, to Belleplaine Boys School.

At the age of six, Hunte would play cricket for hours on end on dirt tracks around his village, using a coconut palm frond bat and a cork ball wrapped in cloth and twine. As he grew older Hunte realized he had an "extra natural" flair for cricket and he set out to develop it. He read cricket books, made notes, studied photographs of great cricketers and practised technical skills in front of a mirror. His school headmaster encouraged Hunte by giving him a shilling every time he made twenty-five runs or more, leading Hunte to joke that he became a professional at an early age.

Conrad Hunte showed the first glimpses of his talent when he was selected for his school's First XI at the age of only ten. He was offered a place with the elite Empire Cricket Club in Division 1 of the Barbados Cricket Association, the home club of his cricketing idol Everton Weekes. But there was little first-class cricket in the West Indies at the time and his career was slow to progress.

Hunte's father was obsessed with his children being well educated and he told Conrad at the age of fourteen that he would 'beg, borrow or steal' to get them all a good education. While acknowledging that his father meant well, Hunte was already convinced that he would 'one day be somebody in the cricket world', and that once that happened he would repay his father's debts and give his parents a comfortable home.

As a teenager, Hunte had two experiences which affected his future. The first was when he read the quotation, 'I expect to pass through this world but once. Any good, therefore, that I can do or any kindness that I can show to any fellow creature, let me do it now. Let me not defer or neglect it, for I shall not pass this way again.'" Hunte was convinced that was what he wanted to do and that he would do it through cricket. The second experience was his confirmation into the Church of England at the age of fifteen. He expected something dramatic to happen, like the 'tongues of fire' settling on the heads of the early Christians, but nothing happened. To cover the fact that he still felt stuck in his 'sinful' ways, he threw himself even more into cricket.

The founding of the Belleplaine Sports and Social Club in 1948 gave Hunte the opportunity to play cricket in the BCL, against men. As the result of a successful 1951 season for Belleplaine, Hunte was selected for the BCL in its annual game against the BCA at Kensington Oval. His graduation in this game to an opening batsman was pure chance. His captain had asked Hunte to open the batting as no one else seemed keen to face local fast bowler, Carl Mullings. Despite sitting on a 'pair' and being a middle-order batsman, Hunte agreed to open. After being dropped second ball by Denis Atkinson, he went on to score 137 not out, becoming the first player to score a century in the annual BCL v BCA matches. Hunte was then selected to play for the Barbados side against Trinidad alongside his hero Everton Weekes and Clyde Walcott. In his first match for Barbados he opened the innings with Roy Marshall and scored 63.

Conrad Hunte made his Test debut in January 1958 against Pakistan at his home ground, Kensington Oval. He opened the batting with Rohan Kanhai, the first of his thirteen opening partners for the West Indies, hit the first two balls he faced for fours and went on to score 142 on debut. In the 3rd Test of the same series Hunte made 260, including a 2nd wicket partnership of 446 with Garry Sobers, which was then the second highest partnership in Test history. In the 4th Test Hunte made another century, finishing his debut Test series with 622 runs at an average of 77.8.

Hunte became the West Indies' regular opening batsman for the next nine years, of which he was vice-captain for eight. He was the West Indies' most consistent and reliable opening batsman during the late 1950s and early 1960s and the West Indies won seven of the ten Test series in which he played. Wes Hall recalls Hunte making centuries on an Australia tour with perfect technique on bad wickets, when everyone else around him was failing.

Conrad Hunte played a major role in the West Indies' series win in England in 1963, curbing his naturally aggressive instincts to help build a solid platform. He played a dogged eight and a half hours' innings of 182 at Old Trafford, helping the West Indies to a ten-wicket win. In the final Test the West Indies were set 253 to win in the fourth innings, with over two days to play. Hunte scored 108 not out to take the West Indies to an eight-wicket victory and a 3–1 series win. Hunte finished the series with an average of 58.9, the highest of the West Indies batsmen, and was selected as a *Wisden* Cricketer of the Year for 1964.

In the 5th Test against Australia at Port of Spain in 1965, Hunte scored an unbeaten 60 and carried his bat through the innings; only the second West Indies batsman at the time, after Garry Sobers, to have done so. Hunte scored 550 Test runs in that series at an average of 61.1, including six fifties in ten innings. That was a record for the highest series aggregate without a century, until English opening batsman Mike Atherton scored 553 in a six-Test series against Australia in 1993.

Garry Sobers recounted a story of the West Indies team being caught in a riot during the 2nd Test at Calcutta in 1967. A policeman had lashed at a spectator with his baton, drawing blood, and the enraged spectators retaliated by setting fire to the stands and anything else they could lay their hands on. In the midst of the pandemonium, Hunte went to the top of the pavilion to take down the West Indies flag and save it from being damaged. In response to Hunte's request for help Sobers replied, "You must be mad," and Hunte proceeded to take it down on his own.

Hunte considered that the 1960/61 West Indies tour of Australia presented a test more profound to him than anything he had encountered on the cricket field. As part of Frank Worrell's drive to build good public relations on the tour, Hunte gave a speech on an Adelaide radio programme titled *Out of Darkness into Light*, which traced the history of the West Indies through colonization and the slave trade and related how, through the dark days of slavery, Christian missionaries had offered a ray of hope in the chasm of despair. The flood of letters Hunte received praising him for his Christian work had the unexpected effect of causing him to anguish as to how he had 'used cricket for fame and fortune and treated God as a convenience to suit [his] whim and fancy.' Hunte felt as though he had actually made a mess of his life and plunged himself deeper into cricket. A few weeks later, Hunte met James Coulter, a key figure in the Moral Re-Armament movement. Coulter and his colleagues so impressed Hunte that he joined the movement and dedicated the rest of his life to its mission.

Conrad Hunte retired from cricket in 1967. In 1998 he was made a Knight of St Andrew of the Order of Barbados and in 1999 was elected to the presidency of the Barbados Cricket Association. He died two months later at the age of 67, while in Australia to speak as a Christian ambassador at a Moral Re-Armament conference.

Seymour Nurse

> My aim was always to play for Barbados and the West Indies, and having achieved this I was satisfied. Life has been good and I must say I'm happy; I played for my people and they showed me great respect.

Born: Saint Michael, Barbados, 1933
Tests: 29 (1960–1969)
Runs: 2,523
Average: 47.60
100s/50s: 6/10
Top score: 258

A powerfully built man, Seymour Nurse was a forceful and aggressive stroke-maker who batted mostly in the middle-order and occasionally as an opener. He liked to play shots early in his innings, sometimes to his detriment. His stroke-play was attractive, if sometimes unorthodox, and he was a superb driver off the back foot. Nurse credited his Empire Cricket Club teammate Everton Weekes for his success in cricket, telling *Wisden* that Weekes made him into a first-class cricketer; a batsman able to get a line on the ball to know precisely where to hit it.

Nurse attended St Stephen's Boys School, where he excelled in both football and cricket. A severe leg injury brought an end to his football career along with advice from his father to stay in cricket and quit football. He started his cricket career in the Barbados Cricket League, playing for the Bay Street Boys' Club; the same club at which Garry Sobers and Conrad Hunte played as young men. He then progressed to the elite Barbados Cricket Association competition, joining the famous Empire club. It was at Empire that Nurse met Everton Weekes, who was to become a major influence in Nurse's cricketing life.

Seymour Nurse did not play for Barbados until he was twenty-five years old, making his first-class debut against Jamaica in 1958. The following year he scored 213 against the touring England team, sharing a 306 run partnership with Garry Sobers. As the West Indies already had so many good middle-order batsmen, Nurse was forced to wait in the wings for some years, finally making his Test debut against England in the 3rd Test of the 1959/60 series. Nurse was called into the Test team as a result of an injury to Frank Worrell and as he had only one bat at the time, held together with tape,

English all-rounder Trevor Bailey presented him with one of his own bats before the match.

Feeling confident after his earlier double-century against the English tourists, Nurse hit the first ball he faced in Test cricket for four, going on to score what was described as a 'sparkling' 70. In later years Nurse lamented that inexperience had cost him a certain century. In 1966 he scored his maiden Test century in the 4th Test against Australia, on his home ground of Kensington Oval. Responding to a large first innings total set by Australia, featuring a record 1st wicket partnership of 382 between Bob Simpson and Bill Lawry, Nurse scored 201 runs.

At the age of thirty-two, Nurse played a leading role in the West Indies' 1966 tour of England, scoring 501 Test runs at an average of 62.6, including a record 5th wicket stand with Garry Sobers at Leeds. He passed 50 five times in the five-Test series.

In 1967, Nurse was named a *Wisden* Cricketer of the Year, *Wisden* commenting that, "[Nurse] may have got himself out at times by going for runs too soon but what a delight it was to witness the power and fluency of his strokes when things did go right."

Seymour Nurse retired from Test cricket at the peak of his powers, scoring 558 runs in his last series against New Zealand, at an average of 111.6, including a double-century in his last Test innings. Many considered that Nurse retired prematurely, Clayton Goodwin being of the view that he could have taken the West Indies unscathed into the 1970s.

Nurse's last Test innings of 258 is the highest score for any individual in a Test innings at Christchurch and is the highest score by a batsman in his final Test innings. After his retirement Nurse served as an administrator and coach for the BCA.

Charles Christopher Griffith

Born: Saint Lucy, Barbados, 1938
Tests: 28 (1960–1969)
Wickets: 94

Bowling average: 28.54
5 wickets in innings: 5
Best bowling: 6/36

Charles (Charlie) Griffith started playing club cricket at a young age, at which time he was a spin bowler. On a whim during one game he switched to fast bowling, took 7 wickets for 1 run, and never went back to bowling spin.

Griffith told Grantley E Edwards that a man had to be tough in Barbados to survive in cricket. The game was very competitive at all levels and only the mentally strong survived at the top. The very fact of being a black man playing a game dominated by the white plutocracy in BCA First Division made Griffith tough.

Charlie Griffith formed a lethal Test bowling partnership with Wes Hall. Due to his height of 193 centimetres and his speed, Griffith was very difficult to play. His performance on the West Indies tour of England in 1963, when he took 32 Test wickets at an average of only 16.2 and helped the West Indies to win the series, marked him down as one of cricket's outstanding fast bowlers.

Griffith explained to Edwards that he would assess batsmen individually and if the wicket was lacking in pace he bowled 'line and length'. His usual method was to attack the batsman so that he had as short a time at the wicket as possible. He would deliver from wide of the crease and then from close to the stumps, advance down the wicket to remind the batsman that a bouncer was due, or bowl one ball medium-fast and follow it with his fastest ball. This was in contrast to the English method of containment where one just bowled line and length, and thus it was difficult for the batsman to settle in the sense that he never knew what Griffith had up his sleeve.

Charlie Griffith was not as extroverted as Wes Hall and became more introverted when he was accused (unfairly in the eyes of some West Indian players and spectators) of a suspect action when bowling his faster ball. But his professionalism was reflected in the fact that he would wake at 3.00 am to go for a long run and his diet consisted of all natural and organic food. Goodwin believed that the English batsmen in 1963 became so focused on Griffith's allegedly illegal bouncer that they dropped their guards against his more lethal slower yorker, with which he reaped a harvest of wickets. The result was that Griffith, more than Hall, dominated the summer of 1963. In that year Griffith topped the season's averages with 119 first-class wickets at the outstanding average of 12.8, resulting in him being selected as a *Wisden* cricketer of the year in 1964.

John Goddard

Born: Saint Michael, Barbados, 1919
Tests: 27 (1948–1957)
Runs: 859
Average: 30.67
100s/50s: 0/4
Top score: 83 n.o.
Wickets: 33
Bowling average: 31.81
5 wickets in innings: 1
Best bowling: 5/31

John Goddard was an attacking left-handed batsmen and a right-arm medium pace bowler who captained the West Indies in 22 Tests, of which 8 were won, 7 lost and 7 drawn. He made his first-class debut when he was only sixteen years old and played twenty years of first-class cricket for Barbados, from 1936 until 1958.

Being white and wealthy, Goddard was earmarked for the West Indies' Test captaincy at an early stage. George Headley had been appointed as captain for the 1st Test against England in Barbados in 1948, the first Test match played by the West Indies after the end of the Second World War and the match in which Everton Weekes and Clyde Walcott made their Test debuts. Headley was not available for the 2nd Test as he had suffered a back strain in the previous match, so Gerry Gomez was appointed captain. Goddard was appointed captain for the 3rd Test, which the West Indies won by 7 wickets and for the 4th Test, which they won by 10 wickets. Goddard was then captain on the tours of India in 1948/49, England in 1950, Australia in 1951/52 and England in 1957.

John Goddard scored more runs and more centuries in the Goodwill Tournaments of the war years than any other West Indian cricketer. Between 1942 and 1947 he scored 1,219 first-class runs for Barbados at an average of 67.7, including five centuries. His highest score was 218 not out against Trinidad in the 1943/44 season, when he and Frank Worrell shared an undefeated 4th wicket partnership of 502 in 404 minutes.

Goddard led the West Indies to series victories against England in 1947/48 and India in 1948/49, but his greatest triumph as captain was leading the West Indies to a 3–1 series victory on the 1950 tour of England. In their three previous tours of England the West Indies had never won a Test match. By the end of the 1950 tour Goddard had captained the West Indies in eleven Tests, winning six and losing only one.

The 1951/52 tour of Australia resulted in a 4–1 win to Australia and Goddard's captaincy was beginning to arouse dissent. Goddard had always encouraged his players to give him advice, but some players felt that he had not been open in acknowledging that he had received such advice. Frank Worrell was annoyed that various factions within the team, unfairly in his eyes, began to withhold advice and assistance from Goddard.

Negative comments from some of those players after the Australian tour resulted in long-standing divisions within the West Indies team. Nevertheless, Goddard was selected as captain for the 1957 tour of England, which the West Indies lost 0–3. In the 3rd Test the West Indies were 6/194 when Goddard joined Cammie Smith. The two shared a partnership of 154, of which Goddard scored 61, which left England too little time to win. John Goddard captained Barbados until his retirement in 1958, after which he served as a Test selector.

Denis Atkinson

Born: Christ Church, Barbados, 1926
Tests: 22 (1948–1958)
Runs: 922
Average: 42.33
100s/50s: 1/5
Top score: 219
Wickets: 47
Bowling average: 35.04
5 wickets in innings: 3
Best bowling: 7/53

Denis Atkinson encouraged the young Garry Sobers to play cricket as a boy, by having Sobers bowl to him in the nets. Atkinson would place a shilling on top of the stumps and tell Sobers that he could have it if he succeeded in knocking it off. Sobers later recalled, "It was through him that I eventually received recognition."

Atkinson was caught in the captaincy dramas that dogged the West Indies in the mid to late 1950s, Richie Benaud recounting that when the Australians arrived in the West Indies for the 1954/55 tour they realized that there was a strange controversy surrounding the issue. There was clearly pressure being applied to have Frank Worrell made captain, but it did not end there. Jeff Stollmeyer was listed to captain the West Indies in the 1st Test against Australia, but the selectors made the odd decision of announcing Atkinson as captain of the West Indies team to tour New Zealand, twelve months hence. The selectors then proceeded to announce that Atkinson would be Stollmeyer's deputy in the series that was about to commence against Australia. On top of that, the side contained Weekes, Worrell and Walcott, all of whom were capable of captaining the West Indies and all of whom had been overlooked, even as vice-captain.

To cap off this unusual state of affairs, on the day before the start of the 1st Test at Sabina Park, Jeff Stollmeyer injured his hand in unlucky circumstances. The West Indies players were training in the nets when one of them hit a ball towards the stand. Seeing that it might hit one of the spectators, Stollmeyer caught the ball and sprained his right forefinger. Denis Atkinson was now captain.

Benaud said of Atkinson:

> I had met Denis in Australia in 1951/52 and liked him. He was a very good cricketer, a tough one too, and I found him one of the most approachable and dedicated players I came across in the twelve years I played Test cricket. He was a tough competitor and someone who improved his cricket all the way through the season in the face of personal attacks [...] [but] making Denis captain of the West Indies in 1955 was roughly the equivalent of the Australian Cricket Board making me captain of Australia at the time. No matter what he did, there would be islands and critics who would tear him apart if they could possibly find a reason for doing so; or, if they couldn't find one, invent one.

Benaud jokingly said that the West Indies selectors at this time could only have had a death wish, because for the 2nd Test they announced that Stollmeyer would return from injury as captain, but that vice-captain Atkinson would not play, in favour of selecting the local Trinidadian 'Bunny' Butler.

Further captaincy dramas ensued in the 3rd Test in Guyana, when captain Stollmeyer badly tore shoulder ligaments when he fell in attempting to field a ball near the boundary edge. He would take no further part in the series and Atkinson was selected again as captain for the final Test in Barbados.

Despite the criticisms against him, the Barbados Test would prove to be Atkinson's finest moment, as he and fellow Bajan Clairmonte Depeiaza proceeded to share a world-record 7th wicket partnership of 347. Atkinson scored 219, the highest score at that time by a West Indies captain. Benaud later stated, "Atkinson's was, considering the circumstances, one of the finest and most courageous exhibitions of batting and character I had seen, and have seen to this day."

Frank McDoland King

    Born: Saint Michael, Barbados, 1926
    Tests: 14 (1948–1957)
    Wickets: 29
    Bowling average: 39.96
    5 wickets in innings: 1
    Best bowling: 5/74

Frank King opened the bowling for the West Indies in three consecutive series. His best wicket tally was in his first series against India in 1953, when he took 17 wickets at an average of 28.2 to finish second behind Alf Valentine. King tended to bowl with hostility and injured several batsmen, but *Wisden* commented that he tended to overuse the bouncer.

King played for Barbados from 1947 to 1957, except for the 1950/51 season when he played for Trinidad. His contribution to Bajan cricket went beyond his humble Test figures. As a member of the Combermere School's ground staff he made a deep impression upon the young Wesley Hall, who worked hard to emulate King's classical fast bowling action. King tended to be susceptible to injury and retired from first-class cricket in 1957, whereupon he moved to England and played league cricket in the Birmingham League.

Eric St Eval Atkinson

    Born: Barbados, 1927
    Tests: 8 (1948–1957)
    Wickets: 25
    Bowling average: 23.55
    5 wickets in innings: 1
    Best bowling: 5/42

Eric Atkinson was the younger brother of Test captain Denis Atkinson and, coincidentally, his debut Test was Denis's last Test. In his second game, at Sabina Park a month later, Atkinson took 5 for 42 (and 8 for 78 in the match), his best bowling performance. Unfortunately, it was somewhat overshadowed by Garry Sobers' world record Test score of 365 not out. A tearaway bowler in his youth, Atkinson didn't have much success when he first played for Barbados, taking three wickets in his first nine matches. But he settled into bowling fast-medium swing when he got into the Test team and was rumoured to have used reverse swing before anyone had a name for it. Atkinson was chosen to tour the subcontinent a year later and, in his last Test, helped the West Indies to victory at Lahore by taking 3 for 15, as Pakistan were bowled out for 104.

Cyril Clairmonte Depeiaza
>Born: Saint James Parish, Barbados, 1928
>Tests: 5 (1948–1957)
>Runs: 187
>Average: 31.16
>100s/50s: 1/0
>Top score: 122
>Catches/stumpings: 7/4

Clairmonte 'Leaning Tower' Depeiaza's international career may have been brief, but he shared a world record 7th wicket partnership of 347 with fellow Bajan Denis Atkinson in the 4th Test against Australia at Barbados in May 1955, of which he made 122; his only first-class century. When Depeiaza joined Atkinson at the crease the West Indies were 147 for 6 in reply to Australia's 668. In an epic stand, the pair batted for the whole of the fourth day. Their partnership still stands as a Test record.

Cammie Wilberforce Smith
>Born: Saint Michael, Barbados, 1933
>Tests: 5 (1960–1962)
>Runs: 222

Average: 24.66
Top score: 55
Catches/stumpings: 4/1

Cammie Smith was a fearless, attacking batsman who excelled against quick bowling and an accomplished wicket keeper. He made his first-class debut at the age of eighteen against British Guiana, scoring 80. In his next match against Jamaica he made 140 out of a stand of 243 for the 2nd wicket with Conrad Hunte. His top Test score of 55 was scored in the 3rd Test against Australia in 1961, when he shared a 4th wicket partnership of 101 with Frank Worrell in only 67 minutes. His top score in first-class cricket was 140 against Trinidad in 1962/63, during a 2nd wicket partnership of 318 with Seymour Nurse. After retiring from cricket he managed various West Indies sides, became an ICC match referee and remained closely associated with the development of the game in Barbados.

Roy Edwin Marshall
Born: Saint Thomas, Barbados, 1930
Tests: 4 (1951–1952)
Runs: 143
Average: 20.42
Top score: 30

Roy Marshall was named as one of *Wisden*'s cricketers of the year in 1959. He made his first-class debut for Barbados at the age of only fifteen and scored 1,117 first-class runs on the 1950 tour of England, although he did not play in any of the Test matches.

Ernest Eytle described Marshall as one who 'lived for cricket' and never minded talking about the game. His performances in Barbados left his peers in no doubt that he would one day be a great player. He was lost to West Indies cricket after the 1950/51 tour to Australia, as he had to make a decision either to accept an offer to play for Hampshire or await selection by the West Indies against some tough opposition.

Michael Robyn Bynoe

Born: Saint Michael, Barbados, 1941
Tests: 4 (1959–1967)
Runs: 111
Average: 18.50
Top score: 48

Robyn Bynoe had played only two first-class matches when he was selected for the West Indies tour of India and Pakistan in 1958/59, at the age of eighteen. He had a good tour, scoring over 500 runs. But on his return he all but disappeared from first-class cricket, playing eight matches for Barbados in the next six seasons. In 1965/66 he scored 251 runs at 62.8, enough to win him a place on the 1966/67 tour to India, where he opened the batting with Conrad Hunte in three Tests. But he was unable to repeat the successes of his first trip to the sub-continent, as he struggled against spin bowling.

Bynoe preferred fast bowling. While some thought he would have made a good opening partner for Conrad Hunte on the 1963 and 1966 tours of England, he was not selected. He continued to score solidly for Barbados, averaging 70.00 in his final season in 1971–72. Bynoe scored a total of 3,572 first-class runs at an average of 41, including a highest score of 190 against Trinidad and Tobago.

Peter Douglas Lashley

Born: Christ Church, Barbados, 1937
Tests: 4 (1960–1962)
Runs: 159
Average: 22.71
Top score: 49

A middle-order batsman who became an opener later in his career, Peter Lashley was part of the West Indies squad on the 1960/61 tour of Australia, on the back of a good hundred for Barbados against British Guiana the season before. He played in the first (the famous tied Test) and last Tests of the series, scoring 78 runs in four innings. His next chance came when he toured England in 1966, where he played in the 3rd and 4th Tests. At Nottingham he scored a patient 49, but failed at Leeds and was dropped, never to return. It was scant reward for one of Barbados's most talented batsmen. In a seventeen-year first-class career he scored 3,994 runs at 48.7 for Barbados, including 2,736 at 55.8 in the Shell Shield with six hundreds. He was also an outstanding close fielder.

Michael Campbell Frederick

Born: Saint Peter, Barbados, 1927
Tests: 5 (1960–1962)
Runs: 30
Average: 15.00
Top score: 30

Michael Frederick's career was one of brief opportunity. An opening batsman, he played one match for Barbados in 1944/45 as a seventeen-year-old. He played twice as an amateur for Derbyshire in 1949 and then twice for Jamaica, both against the touring MCC side, in 1953/54. Frederick made fifties in both matches, and was drafted into the side for the first Test where he scored 0 and 30. That was his sixth and last first-class appearance.

David Walter Allan

Born: Christ Church, Barbados, 1937
Tests: 5 (1962–1966)
Runs: 75
Average: 12.50
Top score: 40 n.o.
Catches/stumpings: 15/3

David Allan was considered by some to be the finest wicketkeeper produced by Barbados before the emergence of David Murray in the 1970s. He made an impressive Test debut against India in Barbados, scoring 40 not out and making five dismissals. However, as he was competing against the likes of Jackie Hendricks of Jamaica and Deryck Murray of Trinidad, his Test opportunities were limited. Allan toured England with the West Indies in 1963 and 1966, but was the reserve wicketkeeper on both occasions.

EIGHT

The Legacy of the Bajan Greats of the 1950s

Another aspect I loved about playing with him [Sobers] in my early days with Barbados was the knowledge he gave you. I would sit in the dressing room when he talked about cricket, along with people like Clyde Walcott, Everton Weekes and Conrad Hunte, and I would just marvel at what they had to say. You dare not speak while they were talking cricket. These were enlightening and gratifying times for me. I don't know if that happens today but I would hope so for the sake of the young players.

Gordon Greenidge

Greenidge, in particular, appeared to have combined the techniques of Weekes with the savagery of Walcott – especially in his approach to such strokes as the cut and the hook.

Keith Sandiford

At school we had Seymour Nurse and Everton Weekes as the main coaches, and sometimes Manny Martindale. We knew they were great players and we all wanted to get as far as they'd done. It was Charlie [Griffith] who made me change my action. I used to deliver with a round-arm double swing which he said would not do at all. In a few months I was doing it the correct way.

Joel Garner

Four Bajan test players who had the opportunity of learning from their great countrymen of the 1950s were Gordon Greenidge, Joel Garner, Desmond Haynes and Malcolm Marshall. All four had long Test careers and made huge contributions to the West Indies sides of the golden era from 1980 to 1995, when the West Indies were unbeaten for an incredible 29 Test series.

Gordon Greenidge
   Born: Saint Peter, Barbados, 1951
   Tests: 108 (1974–1991)
   Runs: 7,558
   Average: 44.72
   100s: 19
   Top score: 226

Gordon Greenidge and Desmond Haynes formed the most successful opening batting partnership in West Indies' Test cricket history, scoring 6,482 runs while batting together, the third highest total for a batting partnership. They shared 16 century partnerships, four of which were in excess of 200. And they still hold the record for the highest West Indian 1st wicket partnership: 298 against England at St John's, Antigua in 1989/90.

Greenidge scored 500 runs in a Test series three times; against England in 1976 and 1984 and against Pakistan in 1976/77. He scored four Test double-centuries, including two in the 1984 series against England, and scored three consecutive Test centuries in the 1976 series against England. He featured in 46 century partnerships for the West Indies; 22 of them being opening partnerships.

Gordon Greenidge was born Cuthbert Lavine in 1951 and lived the early years of his life in his birthplace, Barbados. At fourteen he moved to London to live with his mother and her new husband, whose name was Greenidge. By the age of fifteen he was working and cared more for rugby than cricket. His cricketing break came when he was selected for the young Berkshire cricket side, although he still believes that the only reason he was selected was because he was West Indian. He was chosen again in the next year and made a century against Wiltshire. His name was then recommended to Hampshire, the county side he would represent for eighteen seasons.

Greenidge was selected as a *Wisden* Cricketer of the Year in 1977. Clayton Goodwin considered him to be the most exciting batsman in the world, describing him as one of the very few to persuade a pass-carrying reporter to pay the admission fee at the turnstile if there were no other way of watching him perform.

Desmond Haynes said of Greenidge:

> I would never try to outdo Gordon. I wanted to make sure that our batting partnership was a long one. I don't mean the number of runs we put on in an innings, I mean the number of Tests we played. If he made 89 and I got 11, then it was a hundred partnership and I would be picked in the next game. I was happy to play second fiddle. I always thought Gordon was a better player than I was. He was a more complete player.

In Sydenham's *In a League of their Own,* twenty-six of the one hundred contributors selected Gordon Greenidge as an opening batsman in their greatest side, and Greenidge was selected in the final All Time World XI. South African fast bowler Allan Donald rated Greenidge as the most aggressive batsman he had ever seen and former West Indies captain Richie Richardson rated him as the most technically accomplished.

Desmond Haynes

It's so beautiful to see the hook shot played well…I wanted people to bowl short at me. It was like a half-volley, a four ball.

Desmond Haynes

Born: Saint James, Barbados, 1956
Tests: 116 (1978–1994)

Runs: 7,487
Average: 42.29
100s: 18
Top score: 184

Desmond Haynes featured in forty century partnerships for the West Indies, eighteen of them being opening partnerships. Haynes scored three consecutive Test centuries in 1990/91, two against England and one against Pakistan. Three times in his Test career Haynes carried his bat through an innings; against Pakistan in 1986/87, England in 1991 and Pakistan again in 1992/93.

Tony Cozier once commented that Gordon Greenidge was fortunate to have Desmond Haynes as an opening partner. Whereas Conrad Hunte had to open with thirteen different partners in his Test career, Greenidge had the advantage of opening with only two, Roy Fredericks and Haynes, and his partnership with Haynes lasted for thirteen years.

Greenidge must have appreciated that fact, because when asked to participate in Sydenham's project he paid Haynes the tribute of selecting him as one of the opening batsman in his World XI, partnering Sunil Gavaskar. Greenidge described Haynes as a player who preferred to dominate and who looked to set the pace of how he wanted to play. Former England opening batsman and wicketkeeper Alec Stewart also selected Haynes in his World XI as did Wasim Akram, who described Haynes as a very difficult batsman to bowl at. That was high praise from a bowler considered by many to be one of the greatest of the modern era, and who was himself selected as one of the bowlers in Sydenham's *All Time World XI*.

Desmond Haynes was selected as a *Wisden* Cricketer of the Year in 1991.

Joel Garner
Born: Christ Church, Barbados, 1952
Tests: 58 (1977–1987)

Wickets: 259
Bowling average: 20.97
5 wickets in innings: 7
Best bowling: 6/56

After the glut of great Bajan batsmen in the 1950s, the Bajan cricket stars were, in the main, fast bowlers. Since 1960, Barbados has produced five fast bowlers who have taken 90 or more Test wickets: Wes Hall, Charlie Griffith, Vanburn Holder, Joel Garner and Malcolm Marshall. Two of them, Marshall with 376 Test wickets and Garner with 259, rank among the greatest fast bowlers from any country and any era.

Attending Foundation School, Garner was coached by former Bajan and West Indies greats Seymour Nurse, Wesley Hall and Charlie Griffith. Because competition was so tough in Barbados, Garner didn't make his first-class debut until he was twenty-three years old. On the 1979/80 tour of Australia Garner headed the bowling averages in an attack that included Colin Croft, Michael Holding, Andy Roberts and Collis King.

Garner generated unplayable bounce, due in part to his 203cm height, the ball often rearing alarmingly from barely short of a length. Allied to that was the most devastating yorker the game had seen since that of fellow Bajan pace man Charlie Griffith. Garner dominated the series when the Australians toured the West Indies in 1984, taking 31 wickets.

Of the top Test wicket-takers, few have a lower average than Garner's 20.98 runs per wicket. He took fifty wickets in a calendar year twice and the most wickets for the West Indies in a Test series on five occasions.

Joel Garner was selected as a *Wisden* Cricketer of the Year in 1980 and as one of the Lord's Taverners' fifty greatest cricketers in 1983. In 2010 he was inducted into the International Cricket Council Cricket Hall of Fame and the Federation of International Cricketers' Associations. While honoured to receive the award, Garner is not overly interested in accolades:

I am not going to comment on my bowling or what I did or didn't do. I am happy to have been part of a successful unit, whether it has been a four-pronged pace attack, a three-pronged pace attack or a five-pronged pace attack […] I think we got more fun and more enjoyment out of playing with each other and enjoying each other's company and performing more so than personal statistics.

In 2015 Garner was nominated as a director on the West Indies Cricket Board and re-elected as president of the Barbados Cricket Association. In July 2016 he was appointed as the West Indies' team manager.

Malcolm Denzil Marshall

Even without the ball and only simulating his bowling action, Marshall looks intimidating. He is compact and physically controlled, the ferocity lurking just below the surface.

Michael Manley, describing Malcolm Marshall's warm-up routine

Born: Saint Michael, Barbados, 1958
Died: Bridgetown, Barbados, 4 November 1999
Tests: 81 (1978–1991)
Wickets: 376
Bowling average: 20.94
5 wickets in innings: 22
10 wickets in a match: 4
Best bowling: 7/22

Although not tall for a fast bowler, Malcolm Marshall generated fearsome pace from his quick arm action, bowled a dangerous bouncer and could swing the ball both ways. These factors combined to make him the greatest of all West Indian bowlers and one of the greatest fast bowlers in Test history.

Malcolm Marshall's Test bowling average of 20.9 is the best average of any bowler (from any nation) who has taken 200 or more wickets. On four consecutive occasions he took five wickets in a Test innings. He took fifty wickets in a calendar year three times (1983, 1984 and 1988) and took the most wickets for the West Indies in a Test series on five occasions.

Marshall was educated at St Giles Boys School. He had played only one first-class game before being selected for the West Indies tour of India in 1978/79, in the absence of those players who had chosen to participate in World Series Cricket.

Marshall was named as the Professional Cricket Association's Cricketer of the Year in 1982 and as a *Wisden* Cricketer of the Year in 1983, but his greatest Test performance was yet to come. In the 3rd Test against England at Leeds in 1984, Marshall broke a hand in two places while fielding. At the fall of the ninth West Indies wicket he came out to bat with his arm in plaster, helping Larry Gomes to reach his century. He then bowled the West Indies to a win, decimating England's second innings by taking 7 wickets for 53 runs.

Malcolm Marshall was selected by thirty-five of the contributors to Sydenham's Greatest Test XI challenge. He was named (along with Dennis Lillee and Wasim Akram) as one of the three fast bowlers in the final All Time World XI. Marshall's greatness is reflected in the glowing tributes paid to him by so many of his peers, most of whom rank amongst the best to have played Test cricket.

Conrad Hunte rated Marshall as "the greatest of all the great West Indian quicks of recent times." Martin Crowe (one of New Zealand's finest ever Test batsmen) and Jeffrey Dujon (the West Indies' best wicket keeper-batsman) both called Marshall the greatest West Indian bowler of all time. Former West Indies captain Richie Richardson considered Marshall to be the greatest artist in fast bowling terms that he had ever seen. Pakistan's greatest fast bowling pair Wasim Akram and Waqar Younis rated Marshall as the most intelligent fast bowler they had seen in Test cricket. And West Indian Andy Roberts, rated by former Australian captain Ian Chappell as one of the best fast bowlers he had ever faced, described Marshall as 'one of the greatest fast bowlers that ever lived'.

EPILOGUE

> Cricket…is not an addition or a decoration or some specific unit that one adds to what really constitutes the history of a period. Cricket is as much part of the history as books written are part of the history…Cricket has been a permanent source of serious matters, social growth and differentiation, national unity, and social awareness.
>
> *CLR James*

The Bajan Cricket Knights were not just great cricketers. By all accounts they were great men in terms of character and temperament; admired as much for their integrity and dignity as for their cricketing skills. They were consistently described as good men; humorous, warm-hearted and always ready to offer their help and advice to younger players. They were loved by crowds the world over for their easy-going personalities and good humour and, in some cases, for their deeply held humanitarian and religious convictions. These are the qualities that make great men. These are the qualities CLR James wrote of as being nurtured by the great game of cricket.

APPENDICES

Test Series Played by the West Indies Between 1950–1966

Series	Season	Winner	Won	Drawn	Lost	Total
West Indies in England	1950	West Indies	3	-	1	4
West Indies in Australia	1951/52	Australia	1	-	4	5
West Indies in New Zealand	1951/52	West Indies	1	1	-	2
India in the West Indies	1952/53	West Indies	1	4	-	5
England in the West Indies	1954	Drawn	2	1	2	5
Australia in the West Indies	1955	Australia	-	2	3	5
New Zealand in New Zealand	1955/56	West Indies	3	-	1	4
England in England	1957	England	-	2	3	5
Pakistan in the West Indies	1958	West Indies	3	1	1	5
India in India	1958/59	West Indies	3	2	-	5
Pakistan in Pakistan	1958/59	Pakistan	1	-	2	3
England in the West Indies	1960	England	-	4	1	5
Australia in Australia	1960/61	Australia	1	2	2	5
India in the West Indies	1962	West Indies	5	-	-	5
England in England	1963	West Indies	3	1	1	5

Australia in the West Indies	1965	West Indies	2	2	1	5
England in England	1966	West Indies	3	1	1	5
India in India	1966	West Indies	1	-	-	1
Total	-	-	**33**	**23**	**23**	**79**

Win/Loss Ratios

	Tests won	Tests drawn	Tests lost	Total
Home Tests	13	14	8	35
Away Tests	20	9	15	44
Total	**33**	**23**	**23**	**79**

Test Runs Scored by the Three Ws and the Top Three Australian & English Batsmen from 1948–1958
The Three Ws

Year	1948	1949	1950	1951	1952	1953	1954	1955	1956	1957	1958	Total
Tests	7	3	4	4	4	5	5	5	4	5	8	54
Weekes	878	194	338	224	81	716	487	469	418	195	455	4,455
Walcott	515	70	229	74	212	457	698	827	-	247	385	3,714
Worrell	294	-	539	313	257	398	334	206	-	350	-	2,691
Total	1,687	264	1,106	611	550	1,571	1,519	1,502	418	792	840	10,860
Ave per Test	241	88	276	152	137	314	303	300	104	158	105	201

The English Top Three Run-Scores

Year	1948	1949	1950	1951	1952	1953	1954	1955	1956	1957	1958	Total
Tests	11	7	6	13	7	5	12	10	6	9	7	93
Hutton	759	800	455	903	399	443	825	158	-	-	-	4,742
Compton	776	492	58	469	59	234	830	654	166	205	-	3,943
May	-	-	-	171	206	85	779	759	473	622	497	3,592
Total	1,535	1,292	513	1,543	664	762	2,434	1,571	639	827	497	12,277
Ave per Test	139	184	85	118	94	152	202	157	106	91	71	132

The Australian Top Three Run-Scores

Year	1948	1949	1950	1951	1952	1953	1954	1955	1956	1957	1958	Total
Tests	8	2	6	7	4	8	3	8	9	1	6	62
Harvey	299	235	584	438	258	948	308	696	456	15	327	4,564
Morris	848	66	401	462	131	576	182	307	-	-	-	2,973
Hassett	588	169	315	620	177	600	-	-	-	-	-	2,469
Total	1,735	470	1,300	1,520	566	2,124	490	1,003	456	15	327	10,006
Ave per Test	216	235	216	217	141	265	163	125	50	15	54	161

First-Class Statistics of the Bajan Knights

Sir Frank Mortimer Maglinne Worrell (1 August 1924–13 March 1967)

First-Class Career: 1941/42–1963/64

Batting and Fielding

	Matches	Inns	N.O.	Runs	H.S.	Ave.	100	50	Ct	St
Tests	51	87	9	3,860	261	49.48	9	22	43	-
First-class	208	326	49	15,025	308 n.o.	54.24	39	80	139	-

Bowling

	Matches	Balls	Runs	Wktst	Best	Ave.	Econ.	5w innings	10w match
Tests	51	7,141	2,672	69	7/70	38.72	2.24	2	-
First-class	208	26,740	10,115	349	7/70	28.98	2.26	13	-

Sir Clyde Leopold Walcott (17 January 1926–26 August 2006)

First-Class Career: 1941/42–1963/64

Batting and Fielding

	Matches	Inns	N.O.	Runs	H.S.	Ave.	100	50	Ct	St
Tests	44	74	7	3,798	220	56.68	15	14	53	11
First-class	146	238	29	11,820	314 n.o.	56.55	40	54	174	33

Sir Everton Decourcy Weekes (b. 26 February 1925)

First-Class Career: 1944/45–1963/64

Batting and Fielding

	Matches	Inns	N.O.	Runs	H.S.	Ave.	100	50	Ct	St
Tests	48	81	5	4,455	207	58.61	15	19	49	-
First-class	152	241	24	12,010	304 n.o.	55.34	36	54	124	1

Sir Conrad Cleophas Hunte (9 May 1932–3 December 1999)

First-Class Career: 1950/5–1966/67

Batting and Fielding

	Matches	Inns	N.O.	Runs	H.S.	Ave.	100	50	Ct	St
Tests	44	78	6	3,245	260	45.06	8	13	16	-
First-class	132	222	19	8,916	263	43.92	16	51	68	1

Sir Wesley Winfield Hall (b. 12 September 1937)

First-Class Career: 1955/56–1970/71

Bowling

	Matches	Balls	Runs	Wkts	Best	Ave.	Econ.	5w innings	10w match
Tests	48	10,421	5,066	192	7/69	26.38	2.91	9	1
First-class	170	28,095	14,273	546	7/51	26.14	3.04	19	2

Sir Garfield St Auburn Sobers (b. 28 July 1936)

First-Class Career: 1952/53–1974

Batting and Fielding

	Matches	Inns	N.O.	Runs	H.S.	Ave.	100	50	Ct	St
Tests	93	160	21	8,032	365 n.o.	57.78	26	30	109	-
First-class	383	609	93	28,314	365 n.o.	54.87	86	121	407	-

Bowling

	Matches	Balls	Runs	Wkts	Best	Ave.	Econ.	5w innings	10w match
Tests	93	21,599	7,999	235	6/73	34.03	2.22	6	-
First-class	383	70,789	28,941	1,043	9/49	27.74	2.45	36	1

BIBLIOGRAPHY

Armfield, J: *Absolutely Barbados: One Man's Mission to Discover The Heart and Soul of a Caribbean Paradise*, Miller Publishing Co. Ltd, Barbados, 2015.

Barbados Cricket Association: *Over 120 Years of Organized Cricket in Barbados*, 2012.

Beckles, H & Russell, HD: *Rihanna: Barbados World-Gurl in Global Popular Culture,* The University of West Indies Press, Kingston, 2015.

Benaud, R: *Willow Patterns*, Hodder & Stoughton, London, 1969.

Benaud, R: *Over But Not Out*, Hodder & Stoughton, London, 2010.

Benaud, R & others: *Remembering Richie*, Hodder & Stoughton, London, 2015.

Cardus, N: *Cardus in the Covers*, Souvenir Press, London, 1978.

Chamberlain, M: *Empire and Nation-Building in the Caribbean: Barbados, 1937–1966*, Manchester University Press, Oxford, May 2014.

Constantine, Sir Learie: *The Young Cricketer's Companion*, Souvenir Press, London, 1964.

Coward, M: *Champions: The World's Greatest Cricketers Speak,* Allen & Unwin, Sydney, 2013.

Cozier, T: *The West Indies: Fifty Years of Test Cricket*, Angus and Robertson (UK) Ltd, Brighton, 1978.

Cozier,T: *Ninety Years of Everton Weekes*, CricInfo, 26 February 2015.

Dawson, G & Wat, C: *Test Cricket Lists —The Ultimate Guide to International Test Cricket,* The Five Mile Press, Victoria, Australia, 5th ed., 2006.

Edwards, GE: *Return to Glory*, Caribbean Chapters Publishing Inc., Barbados, 2015.

Eytle, E: *Frank Worrell —The Career of a Great Cricketer*, Hodder & Stoughton, London, 1963.

Goble, R & Sandiford, K: *75 Years of West Indies Cricket*, Hansib, London, 2003.

Golesworthy, M: *The Encyclopaedia of Cricket*, Robert Hale & Co., London, 1972.

Goodwin, C: *Caribbean Cricketers: From the Pioneers to Packer,* Harrap, London, 1980.

Goodwin, C: *West Indians at the Wicket,* MacMillan Publishers Ltd, London, 1986.

Haigh, G: *The Summer Game*, The Text Publishing Co., Melbourne, 1997.

Hall, W: *Pace Like Fire*, Pelham Books, London, 1965.

Hunte, C: *Playing to Win*, Hodder & Stoughton, London, 1971.

Hunt, T: *Ten Cities that Made an Empire*, Penguin, London, 2014.

James, CLR: *Beyond a Boundary*, Yellow Jersey Press, London, 1963.

James, CLR: *A Majestic Innings: Writings on Cricket*, Aurum Press Ltd, London, 1986.

Lister, S: *Fire in Babylon: How the West Indies Cricket Team Brought a People to its Feet*, Yellow Jersey Press, London, 2015. Permission of the Random House Group Ltd.

Malec, M: *Social Roles of Sport in the Caribbean*, Routledge, 1995.

Manley, M: *A History of West Indies Cricket*, Andre Deutsch, London, 1988. Permission of Carlton Books Ltd.

McDonald, T: *Viv Richards – The Authorised Biography*, Pelham Books, London, 1984.

McGilvray, A: *The Game is Not the Same*, ABC Enterprises, Sydney, 1985.

Naipaul, VS: *The Middle Passage*, Vintage, 2012.

Nicole, C: *The West Indies*, Hutchinson & Co. Ltd, London, 1965.

Nicole, C: *West Indian Cricket*, Phoenix Sports Books, London, 1957.

Piesse, K & Main, J: *Calypso Summers*, Wedneil Publications, Melbourne, 1981.

Rippon, A: *Cricket Around the World*, Moorland Publishing, Derbyshire, 1982.

Ross, A: *The West Indies at Lord's*, Eyre & Spottiswoode, London, 1963.

Ross, G: *A History of West Indies Cricket*, Arthur Barker Ltd, London, 1976.

Rutter, O: *A Traveller in the West Indies*, Hutchinson & Co. Ltd, London, 1936.

Sandiford, KAP: *Cricket Nurseries of Colonial Barbados,* The Press University of the West Indies, 1997.

Schomburgk, Sir RH: *The History of Barbados*, Longman, Brown, Green and Longmans, London, 1848.

Sengupta, A: *Wesley Hall – A Gentleman Fast Bowler, Now a Preacher and Knight*, Cricket Country, June 19, 2012.

Shales, M: *Barbados*, New Holland Publishers (UK), London, 2007.

Sherlock, P: *West Indies*, Thames & Hudson, London, 1966.

Sobers, G & Barker, JS: *Cricket in the Sun*, Arthur Barker Ltd, London, 1967.

Stollmeyer, J: *Everything Under the Sun*, Stanley Paul, London, 1983.

Swanton, EW (ed.): *Barclays World of Cricket*, Collins Publishers, London, 1980.

Sydenham, R: *In a League of their Own: 100 Cricket Legends Select Their World XI*, The Derby Books Publishing Company Limited, Derby, 2010.

Tennant, I: *Frank Worrell*, Lutterworth Press, Cambridge, 1987.

The Lord's Taverners Fifty Greatest: Heinemann-Quixote Press, London, 1983.

Thomson, AA: *Cricket: The Great Captains*, Stanley Paul, London, 1965.

Walcott, C: *Island Cricketers*, Hodder & Stoughton, London 1958.

Walcott, C & Scovell, B: *Sixty Years on the Back Foot*, Victor Gollancz, London, 1999.

Walrond, O: *Westminster's Jewel: The Barbados Story*, Amazon, 2015.

Whitington, RS: *Keith Miller, The Golden Nugget,* Rigby Publishers Ltd, Melbourne, 1981.

Wisden Anthology (1940–1963), Queen Anne Press, MacDonald & Co. Ltd, London, 1982.

Worrell, F: *Cricket Punch*, Rupa & Co. (by arrangement with Hutchinson Publishing Group), Calcutta, 1977.

ACKNOWLEDGEMENTS

I wish to thank the following people: Julian Armfield, for always responding to my annoying questions and providing Sir Everton Weekes with a copy of my original manuscript, Sir Everton Weekes, for generously agreeing to read a novice writer's work, and Neville 'Oluyemi' Legall, for allowing me to use his wonderful Barbados-themed artwork.

www.ingramcontent.com/pod-product-compliance
Lightning Source LLC
LaVergne TN
LVHW041253080426
835510LV00009B/718